CAMPAIGN TREATISE

CAMPAIGN TREATISE

A Political Guide to Winning Elections

PRINCE C. AKUBUE

PARTRIDGE

ISBN: Softcover   978-1-4828-8988-8
             eBook   978-1-4828-8989-5

Multiple References taken from National Democratic Institute and J. Brian O'Day

Print information available on the last page.

To order additional copies of this book, contact
Partridge India
000 800 10062 62
orders.india@partridgepublishing.com

www.partridgepublishing.com/india

CONTENTS

DEDICATION

This Campaign Treatise is dedicated to the Almighty
God, the source and supplier of all potential
&
To all aspiring leaders to whom life holds such promise

ACKNOWLEDGEMENTS

This work is a synergistic product of experience and many minds. I am forever grateful to the inspiration and wisdom of many great men and women, and many persons who supported and expanded this work. I give great credits to Jesper Frant, Digital Communications Manager of NDI and National Democratic Institute for International Affairs (NDI), Washington, DC for the permission to cite and quote their work.

I must acknowledge as well the many friends, colleagues, students, teachers and politicians who assisted, advised, and supported this writing effort over the years. I need to express my gratitude and deep appreciation to true friends who have consistently helped keep perspective on what is important in life and shown how to deal with reality.

My amiable appreciation to my spouse, Mrs. Akubue Prince Peace Ifeome for her endearing countenance.

PREFACE

This Campaign Treatise shows how to set a campaign goal for election glory and how to win hearts and minds. But it does more. It probes beneath the surface and points to the real meaning behind, the concept and content, the strategies and secrets of election victory. It explores what works and what does not, and shows how to use principles and strategy in campaigning as a new form of public politics. Applicable to any issue and from any point of view, the book's key steps and tools provide models of motivation, analysis and communication structure.

Practical experience has shown us that in the prelude to an election, a successful campaign must formulate a clear strategy with observable timelines, objectives and responsibilities. The gathering of resources and their subsequent allocation must be planned in such a way as to maximize their effectiveness. Careful preparation ensures time and money are not wasted and that limited reserves are wisely exploited.

Strategy however must always be built on a solid knowledge of the conditions that predominate in a candidate's constituency or district. Attempting to marshal a complex campaign without a deep understanding of the prevailing social, economic and political dynamics of a region is for many candidates a recipe for failure. However, candidate's electoral environment is a prerequisite in campaign planning and victory.

This Treatise is useful for the experienced campaigner and novice alike. This systematic and practical guide shows that campaigning has a key role to play in contemporary politics. While nothing can eliminate the stress of the countdown to Election Day, the proper organization of a political campaign can avoid some unnecessary challenges and hassles.

> *'Campaign organization or team is like soccer team.*
> *When you have finance and finesse, good coach and*
> *players, everyone aims at goal for their glory'.*

CHAPTER ONE

INTRODUCTION

1.1 Preamble

A political campaign can be an exciting experience. A great deal will happen between now and Election Day and with a little forethought and planning, you can be prepared for all the twists and turns and, in many cases, control the situation. This treatise is designed to help you anticipate what will happen and be better prepared.

While the given political landscape is an important factor in any campaign, in many cases the most important factor - the difference between winning and losing - is what goes on inside the campaign.

There are *three types of political campaigns* that have nearly no chance to achieve victory on Election Day due to their own internal failures.

The first is the campaign that does not have a persuasive message to deliver to voters and does not have a clear idea of which voters it wants to persuade. This type of campaign lacks direction from the beginning and the situation will only get worse.

Second is the campaign that has a concise, persuasive message and a clear idea of which voters it can persuade but lacks a reasonable plan of what to do between now and Election Day to persuade these voters. This type of campaign wastes time, money and people as it wanders aimlessly toward Election Day. It is often distracted by the day's events, by things the opponent's campaign does or by things the press says, spending more time reacting to outside factors than promoting its own agenda.

Finally, the third kind of campaign is one that has a clear message, a clear idea of its voters and a plan to get to Election Day but it fails to follow through on the plan, not doing the hard work day after day to get elected. This is a lazy campaign that makes excuses as to why it cannot do what it knows must be done and in the end makes excuses as to why it lost.

The winning political campaign is most often the one that takes the time to target voters; develops a persuasive message and follows through on a reasonable plan to contact those voters.

This book has been developed to assist political parties and candidates in taking these steps to become this type of winning campaign. You should read through the entire handbook once so that you have some understanding of the whole process. You should then go through the handbook step by step, answering all the questions and filling in all the worksheets. In this way, you will have a good start on writing a campaign plan.

A written campaign plan, like the plan for building a house, defines the overall political landscape, the strategy and resources required to get to Election Day. As with construction plans, this Campaign Treatise should serve as a guide to be referred to when questions arise. Progress can be measured against this outline. You could build a house without plans, but you would make a lot of mistakes, you would waste a lot of materials, time, and money and you probably would not be satisfied with the results. It is the same for the political campaign without a written plan. While it is true that every campaign is unique, there are some basic principles that can be applied to any election campaign. This handbook is designed to help you apply these basic principles to your unique campaign.

The basics of any election campaign are deceptively simple. All campaigns must repeatedly communicate a persuasive message to people who will vote. This is "the golden rule" of politics. A political campaign is a communication process - find the right message, target that message to the right group of voters, and repeat that message again and again.

Unfortunately, the actual planning process is much more difficult than simply following one rule. There is much more that goes into the process. This handbook is designed to take the campaign through a step-by-step process to develop a written campaign plan. These steps include:

- ❖ Doing the research necessary to prepare for the campaign.
- ❖ Setting a strategic campaign goal of how many votes are needed to win.
- ❖ Analyzing and targeting voters.
- ❖ Developing a campaign message.
- ❖ Developing a voter contact plan.
- ❖ Implementing that plan.

This campaign treatise cannot give you all the answers to all of the problems your campaign will face. It cannot tell you what your campaign message should be. It cannot tell you who your most likely supporters are. It can suggest to you the most effective methods of contacting voters in your region. What it can do is provide the questions that will help you think through the planning process in a thorough and methodical way.

Therefore, the candidate, the campaign manager or director and all the key advisers should conduct a strategic planning meeting and go through this handbook seriously and rigorously. Your strategic planning session should also result in a written campaign plan. Too often, politicians believe that they hold the winning strategy "in their heads." In reality they have no strategy at all and are wandering aimlessly. Too often the candidate and the campaign manager believe that they are following a single strategy, only to find out later that their opinions about the strategy are completely at odds. A written campaign plan, agreed upon by the candidate, the campaign manager or director and all the key advisors, would help avoid such problems. The rule is simple - if a plan is not written down, no plan exists.

Once you have the written plan, you must follow that plan in a disciplined manner. As with any plan, it is only as good as its implementation. All campaigns must be flexible to changing circumstances, but these changes should be carefully considered and weighed against the original research and strategy laid out in the plan.

A political campaign is an intense experience and, when done correctly, it is also a lot of hard work. There are no tricks or short cuts to winning the confidence of the voters. A political campaign can also be an exhilarating, rewarding and fun experience. To the campaign workers, you should be commended for offering your time and skills to improve the general situation and make democracy work. To the candidates, you should be commended for stepping forward and offering your services to your community. In doing so you not only serve your community, you are contributing to the democratic process as a whole.

In the modern political age, technology is the backbone of any campaign. Well-designed tools will allow your campaign team to share information easily and efficiently, make well-informed decisions, and easily expand as you approach Election Day. Putting the right tools in place can make building your campaign effort that much easier.

1.2 Mission and Vision Statement

The mission every political campaigner is really what he/she are trying or intend to do at the present (running for election) to achieve the set vision tomorrow. The vision must be a broader picture of what the future will be like for the electorate, constituency, district/zone, province or country. After the vision and mission are identified, then a vision and mission statements are developed that are inspiring enough to provide direction for the rest of the strategic and structural processes. The process must be guided by principles (ideologies) and values. The candidate as a leader must establish the vision for the desired results and set the strategy and show commitment for getting there. The candidate role is to motivate and inspire others within considered network to go in the right course for success.

Make a common vision

It is beneficial and rewarding to involve your whole campaigning group in exploring your vision and the changes sought: a shared understanding of the problem will stimulate ideas about possible actions to take, and will also help your group to stay motivated and focused during the campaign. Making a common vision will repose confidence and also help determine ways to monitor, and adjust the implementation of the campaign if necessary.

The campaigner's individual visions of the future should be combined to make a single common vision for the campaign. Discuss in depth which broad actions or changes would resolve the problem you identified, so as to arrive at the world you have envisioned. These required actions should be the main focus of your campaign. Deliberate the scope of your campaign: decide whether it has multiple components (sub-campaigns). If it does, you may choose either to narrow the focus of your campaign or create a multiple-campaign strategy.

1.3   Understand the Campaign's Stakeholders

Stakeholders are people, groups, organizations, or institutions that are connected to or have interest in your issue or can effect your strategy. They may support your campaign, and have the power to change the situation, or even be responsible for the problem identified. They can be internal, connected or external stakeholders. An important task when designing your campaign is to learn as much about the stakeholders as possible. The Campaigner should:

- Comprehend each stakeholder's relationship to the problem and proposed solution
- Define the relationships between different stakeholders
- Determine the ability and willingness of stakeholders to help or hurt your campaign
- Evaluate the roles, responsibilities, interests and concerns of these stakeholders. Are there any potential sources of conflict?
- Identify which of these stakeholders your campaign should concentrate on to create the desired change.
- Assess the importance of the stakeholders that have been identified: are they important to the campaign success, and if so, how? Does their relevance to the campaign project subject to the stage of the campaign (time and goal relevance)?

1.3.1 Mapping Stakeholders and Their Relationships/Relevance

Start creating a map in which entities with a stake or interest in your issue are represented as circles, nodes or star points, and lines between these circles represent relationships/relevance.

- Debate the interaction that is at the root of the problem the campaign wants to address. Who creates the problem? Who is affected by it? How and why are these entities connected to one another?

- Continue taking notes, until you can identify the interaction between entities (nodes) that most represents what you seek to change.
- Identify all of the nodes between which this kind of interaction is happening.
- Place these nodes at the center of your map.
  Identify the relationships of these central nodes with others nodes on your map. This helps to make connection on the relationship(s) that exists. Start locally and move outward regionally, nationally and internationally, if relevant. Depending on your problem, expand your map with two or more levels of nodes (marking these in a clear way):
  o First level: entities with direct contact to the central nodes (family/local)
  o Second level: entities with contact to the first level (regional/national)
  o Third level: nodes with general influence on the issue (international/institutional)
- Next, draw lines representing relationships between these nodes and identify the kind of relationship they have; for example:
  o Common/Mutual benefit
  o Conflict
  o Power/Influence
  o Potential
  o Public Relation(PR)
  o Regulatory

After mapping out as many stakeholders as possible, a graphic representation of your stakeholders' relationships/relevance with your issue is created. Analyze how your stakeholders may help achieve the change(s) you seek.

Moving from stakeholders to targets

Start defining specific objective(s) of your campaign. Consider each stakeholder's level of support and level of influence in the context of your campaign objective(s).

- In simple, active terms, define what would resolve your problem and bring about the change you seek. Your objectives should be specific, measurable, achievable, realistic, and time-bound.
- Using the list of the stakeholders from the previous activity, identify as many as possible who could help achieve your specific objective(s).
- Draw a horizontal and a vertical axis on a large sheet of blank paper. Place the stakeholders as follows:
  - The vertical axis represents their level of influence in achieving the goal of your objective from most influential (top) to least influential (bottom).
  - The horizontal axis represents whether they are likely to oppose (left) or support (right) your campaign.
- After you place all the stakeholders on the paper, identify the most influential entities or individuals as potential primary targets, those who can make the change you seek. Note their level of support or opposition for this change.
- Debate the relationship of these entities to other stakeholders.
- Identify stakeholders who support your campaign and have influence on or relationships with your primary target group. They are your secondary targets, or participant groups, who could become actively involved in helping your campaign accomplish its goals. Pinpoint them on your graph and identify two or three participant groups to concentrate on.

After you have identified the target audiences that your campaign needs to communicate with, and relationships they have with other entities with a stake or interest in the problem, consider what tactics or strategies will best address your target and participant groups? The result is a spectrum of stakeholders, a few of whom you have identified as primary or secondary targets.

  - Active allies: supportive and motivated to achieve your goals/objectives
  - Allies: may benefit from your success
  - Neutral parties: may not be involved or affected currently
  - Opponents: may suffer from your success

o   Active opponents: actively and negatively interfere with your activities.

Now that the stakeholders and their relevance have been identified, there is a need to have a meeting with the stakeholders to help you gain an insight into any possible conflicts of interest and how to identify opportunities to improve your working relationship. Also discuss how they will be involved to achieve your campaign set goals.

CHAPTER TWO

STEP ONE- DATA COLLECTION AND RESEARCH

2.1. Research

The larger part of the activities here is data collection and research to inform your strategy. Of course you need to know what kind of data and information you are looking for. One of the difficult and yet an essential part of preparing for political election campaign is to have in place a winning strategy for a successful campaign. In fact, it requires a lot of hard work and thorough research to develop a winning campaign strategy. This is one of the reasons, many well-meaning candidates ignore the necessity to develop campaign strategies and therefore, run into campaign without it. Some resort to corrupt strategies in an attempt to win an election. Consequently, they are disappointed with the results after much time and resources are exhausted. A thorough research and a well design campaign strategy and implementation plan can help you to:

- ➤ run for public office on a solid foundation
- ➤ be more confident and comfortable in your campaign
- ➤ use your limited time and resources strategically to maximize results
- ➤ to know where you will concentrate your campaign efforts
- ➤ to know what to do and what to avoid
- ➤ to know where the race will go from the beginning

> ➤ to know your position in the race well before the casting of votes and counting
> ➤ to minimize your chances of engaging in corrupt practices in democratic election
> ➤ to promote free and fair election
> ➤ to enjoy your campaign with fun and be more relaxing
> ➤ to increase your chances of winning in the political election campaign and many more.

Every campaign is different and unique. While certain basic principles can be applied to each campaign, it is important to have a complete understanding of the particular situation and the conditions in which your campaign will be waged. At some point in almost every campaign, someone says, "it is different here" or "you're not taking into account our particular situation." "Step One: Research" is where you start and where you take into account the differences and peculiarities of each campaign. It is here that you have the chance to demonstrate just how different your situation really is.

The first step in developing a winning strategy must begin with a realistic assessment of the political landscape in which you will be running. It is true that you can never know everything about your district or constituencies, your opponents and the voters. However, by using your time wisely and setting clear priorities, you will be able to compile the kind of information you need to develop a good strategy and be prepared for most events in the coming campaign. There are a number of factors that should be understood as completely as possible as you prepare to write a campaign plan:

> ❖ What is the type of election and what are the rules?
> ❖ Your strength and weaknesses and how this will affect your campaign
> ❖ Voting trend in your electorate, constituency or province over the years
> ❖ Your geographical, social, cultural, political and economic environment
> ❖ Your social, professional, religious and political network
> ❖ Your reasons for running in the election campaign
> ❖ Demographic analysis
> ❖ Total number of eligible voters in the last and current election in the electorate wards, district, local council or government area.

❖ Identifying and establishing your base voters, swing voters and opponent

❖ What are the pressing issues in the community, district or province?

❖ What are the constitutional requirements for this office?

❖ The total number of contestants in the last election and how many will be contesting in the current election.

❖ What are the strength and weaknesses of all the viable opponents?

❖ The winning number in the last election

❖ The total numbers of votes you will require to win in this election and how will you secure these numbers?

❖ What are the human resources issues involved

❖ Your message and your ability to effectively deliver it among others. A careful environmental analysis is key indicators to inform your wining strategies for your campaign.

Each of these points can be expanded into many more questions (as shown below and Appendix B). You will know the answers to some questions immediately and others will require some research. In some cases, you may have to take an educated guess about the answer to a particular question, but you should do this only as a last resort.

It is important for the campaign team to take some time to research the answers to as many of these questions as possible. If you have a large, reliable campaign team, you may want to assign different sections to different members of the team. They can then report their findings to the campaign manager who will be responsible for writing the final campaign plan.

Either alone or as a team, it is important that you set and stick to a time limit for doing the research. There will always be more information you can gather, but this will only delay the use of the information you already have in developing your strategy.

In some cases, this type of research may benefit from more scientific methods of obtaining the data, such as political polling or focus groups. You will need to determine what resources are available to you and whether they are worth the expense of time and/or money. On a larger campaign where thousands of money will be spent on advertising, you would be foolish not to spend a fraction of that amount to see if the message of that advertising will work.

Appendix B provides a detailed list of the following questions. You are encouraged to answer all of these questions carefully. While a few particular questions may not apply to your zone, the complete list is designed to make you think about what is needed to develop a clear strategy.

Generating Alternatives - After environmental scanning is done, it is wise to analyze all the issues, challenges, opportunities, threats and explore all possible ways to address them. Some issues may present an opportunity to adopt new procedures. The fundamental part of alternatives is to create "differentiation". Looking at what others are doing and compare with what you are doing and look at how you can do it differently and effectively from the rest. Differentiation is the key to sustainable competitive advantage. You will need to approach campaign differently from the conventional.

Formulating Strategy - Strategy is about "what to do" and "what not to do". Strategy defines how you will channel all your resources and energy. Any energy expended elsewhere harms your campaign. Strategy requires the selection of target voters - and with these come competitors. You need to decide about products and services, channels and branding. Thus much of a "strategy" is in large part "marketing strategy". How you market yourself and your policy to voters – consumers effectively.

Performance drivers and implementation - So many strategies fail not because they were bad strategies but because of poor implementation. Critical performance drivers should be identified and action plans developed around them. All the members of the campaign team and supporters must be well informed and every one of them knows what role to play in the election process.

An in-depth analysis and understanding of voters' needs are essential to produce a good campaign strategy. It is necessary to understand the nature and scope of voter's needs, how these needs differ between different groups or individuals, and how these needs are changing. Strategies are therefore market driven.

2.2. Election Rules

It is important to first determine the type of election in which you will be running and what will be the rules of the election. Much of the basic strategy depends on this information.

❖ Is this a legislative office you are seeking or an executive office?
❖ Do you need a majority of the votes to win or a plurality?
❖ Will there be a runoff election?

You should definitely research the laws and, if they are complicated, you may want to ask your political party or a lawyer to draft a memo outlining the most important points. Missing a deadline or violating some part of the law could end your campaign before it has even begun.

2.3. The Area (Constituency/District)

Once you have determined the basic election rules, you should start to gather as much information on the area (district) and the voters as possible.

❖ How large is the constituency or district in which you will be running?
❖ What type of terrain will you have to cover as you campaign?
❖ What type of transportation will you and the voters need to use?
❖ How has the population of the area changed recently?

You need to understand the political landscape in which you will be operating.

• *Who are the **important political players** in the area?*
• How strong are the various political parties in the area?
• Who are the civic and business leaders that can influence the campaign?

Winning the support of a particularly influential leader in the community can often make the campaign much easier.

You also must understand how voters get their information.

❖ What are the local media outlets?
❖ Who are the reporters and what are their deadlines?
❖ How will the election be covered and how does the press view the various candidates?

To develop a comprehensive press strategy, it is important to have as much information on the media as possible.

2.4. The Voters

You will need to break the voters in your constituency/district into manageable groups. This is the basis you will later use to develop a strategy for targeting particular voters.

The following are some of the questions you may want to consider.

+ Is there a voter file or accurate list of all possible voters available to the campaign?
+ What support is there for various political parties?
+ What is the demographic composition of the voters?
+ For example, what are the income levels, education levels, professions, ethnic backgrounds, religious backgrounds, age, gender, etc.?
+ Where do people work, shop and play?
+ What is the geographic break down of the voters?
+ What percentage or how many people live in the city, in the rural areas or in small villages?
+ Do the voters live in single-family homes or apartments?
+ How would you describe your supporters and those voters you hope to persuade?

Voters with similar characteristics may have similar interests and may tend to vote the same way. Seniors will be less interested in schools and more interested in pensions while young mothers will be more interested in schools and less interested in pensions. By determining how many senior citizens there are and how many young mothers there are, you will be better able to target your message to groups that matter to your success.

2.5. Past Elections

Often you can gain valuable information about this election by looking at information from past elections.

❖ Who ran for this position in your constituency in past elections and what were the results?

❖ How many voters turned out for similar elections in the past?

❖ How many votes were needed to win?

You may be able to use this type of information to predict the turnout and baseline levels of support in this election. How did candidates with similar backgrounds and messages fair in past elections? You will want this type of information later when you determine what worked for them and what you will have to do differently to do better than they did.

2.6.   This Election

Next you should look at the factors that will affect this election, namely the various issues that concern voters and other political campaigns, which are being waged in the area.

- What local, regional or national issues are important to voters?
- What will motivate voters to go to the polls?
- How would you describe the voter mood?
- What other races will be on the same ballot?
- Will candidates in other races help or hurt your campaign?
- Is there the opportunity to work with other campaigns in a coordinated manner?
- What effect will other campaigns have on the election?

Your relationship with your party and other candidates on the same ticket will affect your strategy. Your campaign's message should complement, or at least not contradict, the other messages.

2.7.   Our Candidate

The most important factor in your election will be the candidate. During your strategic planning session, you should honestly and candidly judge the strengths and weaknesses of your candidate. As you do this exercise, you should also look at your candidate from the point of view of your opponent. What you may view as a fresh new face with new ideas, your opponent may view as a lack of experience.

You may want to organize your assessment into various sections, such as the candidate's childhood, education, work history, immediate family, and past political positions.

It is important to look for both strengths and weaknesses in all of these areas. By finding weaknesses early, the campaign will be better prepared to deal with them and respond to changes that may come up later in the campaign. Too many candidates have lost because they refused to deal with past mistakes and were caught off guard when their opponents painted the picture of their mistakes in a very unflattering light.

2.8. Viable Opponents

Once you have determined your own candidate's strengths and weaknesses, the next logical step is to repeat the process for your opponents'. If you are facing several opponents, you should determine your strongest competitors for the loyalty of voters you hope to attract. Again, you can organize your assessment into various sections and look for both strengths and weaknesses.

Your opponents will not be forthcoming with information about themselves. You will probably need to do some digging to find reasons for voters to vote against them and for your candidate.

Too often candidates and campaigns view opposition research as looking for the one scandal that will finish off their opponent's campaign. This may happen, but more often what you find is patterns of behavior that you can use to persuade voters to either vote against your opponent or for you. You will use this to create a contrast between your candidate and campaign and your opponents' campaign when you develop your message, but this process is the basis for finding that contrast.

The other mistake campaigns often make, is saying that they do not want to wage a negative campaign. Researching your opponent and waging a negative campaign are two entirely different things. By not taking the time and doing the hard work of opposition research, you forfeit the ability to be prepared for what your opponent will say and do and to build the contrast between yourself and your opponent.

As you gather your opposition research, you must be extremely well organized: list the sources of your documentation, and have a system in place that will allow you to quickly access the information. It will do no good to know something and not be able to provide backup of the information. All of this research should be gathered together in a binder for easy referral and referenced for easy tracking. Being meticulous and organized now will save a lot of time and energy later.

2.9. Worksheet 1: The Political Landscape Assessment

❖ Set aside a few hours for you and your campaign team to do a comprehensive analysis of the political landscape in which your campaign will be operating. Everyone should have a copy of the questionnaire in "Appendix B: Campaign Research Questions."

❖ Answer as many of the questions as possible. If you do not have the answers immediately available, determine where the information can be found and who will be responsible for gathering it. It is important to set a deadline for finding the information. You may want to have a second meeting of the campaign team in a week's time to bring together all the information.

❖ Once you have compiled all the research, create a notebook that will provide the details in an organized fashion and draft a summary of the information that will be used as the basis for your strategy and the written campaign plan.

National Democratic Institute for International Affairs (2009). Political Campaign Planning Manual, A step by step guide to winning elections, Washington, DC: NDI.

CHAPTER THREE

→————————————————←

STEP TWO- SET A GOAL

3.1. Setting a Goal

The ultimate goal of almost every political campaign is to win elected office. What you need to do here is determine what must be done to achieve that victory. Too often campaigns forget to calculate how many votes will be needed to guarantee victory and determining where these votes will come from. They then spend their precious resources of time, money and people trying to talk to the whole population instead of the much fewer voters they will need to win. Here you will reduce the number of voters with whom you need to communicate to a much more manageable size. As part of your research, you should determine the total population of your district, the total number of voters, the expected votes cast, the number of votes needed to win and the number of households in which these voters live. Some of the answers that are needed here require you to look into the future and make some educated guesses. Use your best judgment and the information you have found from past elections.

3.2. What is the Total Population of the Area?

"Total population" is all the people who live in your area. Considering children too young to vote and people not registered in the area, this number should be larger than the total number of voters.

3.3.   What is the Total Number of Voters?

"Total number of voters" is all the voters in the area or zone who are eligible to vote and can possibly vote in this election.

3.4.   What is the Expected Turnout?

"Expected turnout" is the expected votes cast in this election. Not every voter will vote. Often you can determine how many voters will vote by looking at past similar elections. If there was 35% turn out in the last general or city election and there are no added factors at this time to change the situation, you might figure out that about 35% would vote in the city election this time. If on the other hand, there was a 55% turnout in the presidential election and this time the city election is combined with the presidential election, you may want to estimate that 55% will turn out this time.

3.5.   How Many Votes are needed to win?

This is a very speculative number. What you are looking for is the total number of votes needed to guarantee victory in your race. If you need a majority of the votes to win, this would be 50% of turnout plus one vote. In many cases you only need a plurality of the votes cast or more votes for your candidate than any other candidate in the race receives. In the case of multi-candidate races, you may be able to win with 35%, 30%, 25% or less of the vote. It is important to convert this percentage to a real number. How many actual votes will guarantee your victory? You should be conservative and error on the side of too many votes rather than too few.

3.6.   How Many Households do these Voters live in?

You can reduce this group yet again. On average, let us say that there are two voters per household. Some families may have three or four voters living in the same house. Some voters may be single and live alone. Now, if you think that a husband and wife are likely to vote the same way, you can often assume that if you talk to one member of the family, then you can expect to get the second vote. So, how many households will you need to communicate with to receive the number of votes needed to win?

Check it out

How does all this come together? Let us say that your constituency or district has a population of 130,000 people. Of this population, there are 30,000 children below voting age and other non-registered voters, leaving a total number of 100,000 voters. In the last city election, there was 50% turnout of voters, or 50,000 votes cast. You assume it will be the same this time. In a multi-candidate race for local council, the winning candidate received 34% of the vote or 17,000 votes cast. If you figure an average of two voters per household, this would come to 8,500 households.

Now, you cannot assume that every voter you talk with will be persuaded to vote for you. So you should figure to communicating with a larger number of voters in order to receive the votes from 17,000 voters or 8,500 households. Suppose you persuade seven out of every 10 voters you communicate with to vote for you. You will need to talk to 25,000 voters or 13,000 households in order to be assured of support from 17,000 voters or 8,500 households (25,000 x 0.7 = 17,500 and 13,000 x 0.7 = 9,100). It is still a lot easier to talk with and try to persuade 13,000 families than it is to talk to and try and persuade 100,000 people. This whole process is narrowing the group of people you need to persuade down to a much smaller size.

3.7. Worksheet 2: Setting Campaign Goal

Using your research information and your best judgment, answer the following questions and incorporate the answers into your written campaign plan:

- ❖ How many people (not just voters) live in your constituency or district?
- ❖ How many of these people are able to vote in this election?
- ❖ What percentage of these voters do you expect to vote in this election?
- ❖ How many expected voters is this in real numbers?
- ❖ How many candidates will be running for this position?
- ❖ How many of these candidates could be considered serious?

- ❖ If the election were held today, what percentage of the vote do you think each candidate would receive?
- ❖ What percentage of the votes cast will be needed to win?
- ❖ How many votes cast in real numbers are needed to win?
- ❖ On average, how many voters live in one household?
- ❖ Do these voters living in the same household all tend to vote for the same candidate?
- ❖ If they do tend to vote for the same candidate, how many households will you need to receive the support of to guarantee victory?
- ❖ If you talk to ten average voters, how many can you persuade to vote for you?
- ❖ How many households will you need to communicate with for your message to reach enough voters to achieve victory?

National Democratic Institute for International Affairs (2009). Political Campaign Planning Manual, A step by step guide to winning elections, Washington, DC: NDI.

CHAPTER FOUR

STEP THREE- TARGETING THE VOTERS

4.1.   What is Targeting?

The modern (or "new-style") campaign relies on targeting – choosing, in advance, which voters to contact and devoting time and money to increasing the quality and quantity of that contact. Once you decide how many votes you need to win and, therefore how many voters you need to persuade to support your candidate, you need to determine what makes these voters different from other voters who will not support your candidate. This process is called "targeting the voters" or simply "targeting." The point of targeting is to determine which subsets of the voting population are most likely to be responsive to your candidate and focusing your campaign efforts on these groups of voters.

You will remember when you worked on "Step One: Research," you were asked to break voters down into more manageable groups. It was said then that you would use this information when you target particular voters. That time has come.

4.2.   Why Target Voters?

Targeting is important for two reasons. First, you want to conserve those precious campaign resources of time, money and people, and second, you want to develop a message that will best persuade those voters you still need to convince to vote for you.

4.2.1. Conserving campaign resources

If you develop literature for everyone in the constituency and try to shake the hand of every voter in the constituency, then you are wasting a lot of money and a lot of time on people who will not vote for you no matter what you say or do.

If, on the other hand, you can identify a smaller but significant group of voters who will most likely be persuaded by your campaign message. You will then be able to concentrate your efforts on them and you will have more resources to repeat your message over and over again, until it seems that they have no choice but to vote for your candidate.

Suppose, for example, that you decide that you need to communicate with 33% of the voters to win. If you could identify exactly which voters were most likely to deliver that 33%, then your campaign could reach them with one-third of the resources that you would need for an untargeted campaign. Put another way, if your campaign had the resources to reach every voter in the district one time, you could instead target your efforts to reach your most likely supporters three times.

Candidates that do not take the time to target their voters have lost the right to complain about scarce campaign resources.

4.2.2. Persuading target voters

In the next section a good bit of time will be spent discussing your campaign message. Before that however, you need to determine who the best audience for that message will be. This will help you determine what you can say that is likely to persuade them.

An important rule to remember is that as a party or candidate tries to reach a broader and broader audience, then that party's or candidate's message becomes defused and weaker for each part of that audience. Ultimately, the party or candidate that promises everything to everybody has an empty message that no voter will find credible or compelling.

The goal of targeting, therefore, should be to focus your campaign effort on a range of voters that can deliver approximately the same number of votes that you set as your campaign goal in Step Two. If your target audience is too narrow, you will not attract enough votes to win. If your target audience is too broad, your message will become diffused, and candidates with better focus will steal parts of the message - and the electorate - from you.

Generally speaking, there are three types of voters: **your supporters, your opponents' supporters and those voters in the middle who have yet to make up their minds**. Your supporters are those who have already decided to vote for you. Your opponents' supporters are those who have already decided to vote for your opponents. Those voters in the middle who have not yet decided and still need to be persuaded to vote for one or the other candidates are called persuadable voters. It is some portion of these persuadable voters whom you want to target and with whom you want to communicate your message. Remember that a political campaign is a communication process.

4.3.   How to Target Voters

Once you have determined that you need to persuade only about half of the electorate or less to vote for your candidate, you need to figure out what makes your potential voters different from the others. There are two ways to determine this: geographic targeting and demographic targeting. Most campaigns will use some combination of both methods.

4.3.1. Geographic targeting

Geographic targeting is simply determining who will vote for your candidate based on where they live. For example, let us say that candidate "A" lives in town "A" and is well known and liked by her neighbors. Candidate "B" lives in town "B" and is well known and liked by his neighbors. Most of candidate "A's" supporters are going to come from town "A" and she needs to go to town "C" to persuade those residents who are not already committed to a candidate in the race that she is the best candidate. She would be foolish and wasting her time to go to town "B" and try to persuade those residents and neighbors of candidate "B" to vote for her.

This is a very simple example, though there are elections where the targeting is that easy. More often the campaign will have to look at past elections to determine past performance, the Persuadability of the voters and the expected turnout. This can best be done where data can be obtained for past elections down to the ward level.

Past performance is the percentage of votes that your candidate, your party or a similar candidate received in past elections. Wards with high performance contain your most likely supporters. In theory, a campaign should not spend resources on very high-performance wards; after all, it makes little sense to try to persuade voters who will already vote for you. However, most candidates should spend some resources in areas with a history of voting for democratic candidates and parties in order to solidify their base of support before reaching out to other potential supporters.

The Persuadability of voters is the percentage of voters in a ward that do not vote in a consistent way. It is the difference in percentage of votes for similar candidates either in the same election or two consecutive elections. Voters either "split" their vote (vote for candidates of different orientations in the same election) or "shift" their vote (vote for candidates of different orientations over the course of two or more elections).

In a U.S context, "vote splitting" districts would be districts that voted for Democrat Bill Clinton for President and a Republican member of Congress in the same election. In a Russian context, "vote shifting" districts would be districts that voted for a Communist member of the Duma and then voted for President Yeltsin in the next election less than one year later.

It is generally considered that "vote splitters" and the "vote shifters" are the voters most likely to be persuaded by a campaign's efforts. Because of this, most campaigns spend the majority of their effort - posters, door to door, etc. - in precincts with high Persuadability. This strategy makes sense.

Expected turnout can be determined by the percentage of voters who turned out in the most recent similar election. It makes no sense to spend campaign resources on people who will not vote, so your campaign should spend more resources on areas with a history of higher turnout.

Appendix C provides a more detailed look at the methodology used for measuring a ward's "turnout," "performance" and "persuasiveness." You will need to determine which formulas make the most sense in the context of your region or election. Once you have decided upon a formula, you can do the math or enter the ward-level voting data into a computer spreadsheet and determine for each ward a level of turnout, performance, and Persuadability.

You will then be able to rank your district's or constituency's areas, as in the following example:

Area Number	Total Votes	Turnout	Democratic Performance (Average of similar parties)	Persuadability (Percentage that sometimes votes democratic)
35	976	62.5%	43.4%	11.2%
107	1,563	52.7%	41.2%	16.7%
14	1,132	53.4%	35.7%	26.7%
77	875	55.7%	28.3%	12.7%
93	1,343	27.2%	26.5%	29.5%
178	734	60.4%	23.1%	17.3%

Your campaign should plan different tactics for different types of areas or precincts. In this example, the plan may call for a lot of posters or a series of rallies in areas like 35 and 107 in order to solidify a very high democratic base. On the other hand, the candidate may want to personally go door to door in areas like 14 with a high level of "Persuadability." Note that while area 93 also has a very high level of "Persuadability," past turnout indicates that few people living in that area will actually vote and the candidate should not waste their time with inactive voters.

4.3.2. Demographic targeting

Demographic targeting is splitting the voting population into various groups or subsets of the population. These groups can be based on age, gender, income, level of education, occupation, ethnic background or any other distinct grouping. The point of breaking the population down like this is that similar people are likely to have similar concerns and vote for the same candidate.

We can then mix groups into cross-sets or break them down further into subsets of subsets. For example, breaking the population down by gender may give you roughly 50% of population for men and for women (do not assume this is always the case). Working women would be a smaller subset of women. Working women with children would be an even smaller subset of working women. Working women with children are likely to have very particular concerns about childcare that, if your candidate addresses, is liable to persuade a large percentage of them to vote for you. The trick here is for the group not to be so small as to be insignificant.

Our demographic groups

Often when determining which groups will be persuaded to vote for a candidate, you should look for groups to which the candidate belongs. Say the candidate is a 38-year-old, college educated small businessman, married with a son and a daughter in school, living in the largest city in the district. His target groups are going to be young people between the ages of 25 and 40, small business people, and parents with school age children. He is less likely to appeal to groups of the voting population to which he does not belong. He will have less appeal to pensioners, workers with less education, and farmers from the rural part of the zone. If there are enough votes in his target groups to win and he is the best candidate to appeal to these voters, then he need only to communicate a persuadable message to this group throughout the campaign to win.

There are two things that can make this targeting less likely to work. First, the demographic groups he chooses are too small. Second, there are other candidates with similar backgrounds who are appealing to the same group. In both cases, if another candidate is also appealing to this same group or it is not a large enough part of the population to provide the margin of victory, then the campaign needs to look to collateral groups or those groups nearest in interests for further support. In the above example he may want to expand his message to include people with a higher education (usually professionals). He would want to broaden his message to appeal to teachers and doctors, which may work nicely with his message to parents with school age children.

The point of all of this is to do the math and figure out how many voters in a particular group can be expected to vote for the candidate if they hear a message that addresses their concerns. You shouldn't expect to win 100% of the vote of any population but if, with a little effort, you can expect to receive 6 or 7 out of every 10 votes cast, then this is a group of voters with whom you should be in touch.

You will not be able to come up with very precise numbers for these groups (politics, after all, is an art, not a science). However, going through this exercise and determining numbers for your subsets and cross-sets will help you determine whether your targeting strategy is realistic or not.

Their demographic groups

An important part of demographic targeting is determining which demographic groups will not be part of your targeted audience. During your strategic planning session you should, for example, state explicitly "we will not target government workers" or "we will not target young entrepreneurs." This exercise will help you avoid the trap of defining too wide a targeted audience.

It is often easy to determine which demographic groups you are willing to give to your opponents once you have decided which groups are yours. They are the opposite of the groups that you consider to be your best target groups. For example, older male pensioners are going to have the least in common with young working mothers, so if you have targeted one group, you will most likely give the other group to your opponents. It would be very difficult to develop a message that will persuade both groups that you have their interests at heart.

4.4. Problems with Targeting

Again, demographic targeting is not a precise science; even in the best of circumstances, definitions of demographic subsets are fuzzy and overlap with one another. They can be made more difficult by three factors:

> ➢ A large number of candidates in each race, which forces candidates to consider groups from which they will receive much less than half the vote.
> ➢ The lack of available, accurate demographic data.
> ➢ The undeveloped self-identification of individuals as having specific interests based on their demographic characteristics.

Nevertheless, it is important to do this exercise and look at these issues. Many candidates in the past have lost largely due to a failure to define a target audience. Candidates, when asked to identify their audience tended to respond either 1) by naming every demographic subset imaginable, or 2) by saying, for example, "I represent the intelligentsia." In the first instance, they had no target audience because their target audience was everybody. In the second, their target audience was simply too small to bring them victory (the intelligentsia is a relatively minor part of the voting population and is, moreover, claimed by virtually every democratically oriented party).

Bringing it all Together

The following chart provides one model of how to relate targeting to your campaign efforts:

	Likely Voter	**Potential Voter**	**Non-Voter**
Likely Supporter	A Solidify Support Base	D Focus on Motivating to Vote	G Possible motivation effort (last priority)
Potential Supporter	B Primary focus for message communication and persuasion	E Secondary focus for persuasion	H No Program
Unlikely to Support	C Possible Communication (low priority)	F No Program	I No Program

Source: National Democratic Institute for International Affairs (2009).

Explanations

Box A: People who are most likely to vote and are most likely to support you are your base of support. You should, first of all, plan activities to solidify this support.

Box B: Likely voters who are potential supporters are your number one target for your persuasion efforts. Spare no effort on these voters.

Box C: Do not spend too much time on people who aren't likely to support you. In fact, your activities may make it more likely that they will go to the polls and vote for your opponents.

Box D: Likely supporters who are only potential voters must be persuaded to vote. Target these people with motivational messages and a strong Election Day push to make sure as many of them as possible vote.

Box E: Potential voters and supporters are important but not crucial. Focus on them only after you've communicated with Boxes A and B.

Box G: Possible target for motivational efforts but do not spend scarce campaign resources here until you've thoroughly covered the boxes above or if you need these votes to win. Your time, money and people would be better spent above.

Boxes F, H, and I, do not waste efforts on these voters.

4.5.   Voters Analysis

Having determined a target audience for your campaign, you should make an effort to understand the members of this target audience thoroughly. The four areas you should analyze are values, attitudes, issues and desire for leadership qualities.

4.5.1. Values

What are the core values that unite the voters in your target audience? For example, which do they value more?

- Social protection or economic opportunity?
- Personal freedom or societal order? Reform or stability?
- Peace or military security?
- What values do they share with the rest of the population?
- What values set them apart from the rest of the population?

4.5.2. Attitudes

This describes how the voters feel going into the election - either satisfied or angry, feeling better off or worse off. Voters' political attitudes are most strongly anchored by left/right ideology. Understand voter attitude towards political settings through a battery of questions about voters.

- ❖ Are voters optimistic or pessimistic about the future?

❖ Are they trustful or mistrustful of government and other social institutions?

❖ Do they feel better off or worse off now than in the past?

❖ Do they want change or stability?

4.5.3. Issues

What are the important issues that will make voters sit up and take notice of this election? Generally, you should know whether voters are more concerned about economic issues, social issues, or foreign policy issues. Examples of more specific questions to ask might include the following: Is controlling crime more important or less important than it was in the past? Will your position on business investment be important in this election, or will no one care?

4.5.4. Leadership qualities

What qualities do voters most want to see in their leaders?

❖ Are they looking for stable, experienced leadership, or do they want someone young and dynamic who will shake up the establishment?

❖ Would they prefer leaders from the intelligentsia, or do they want leaders who can relate to the concerns of the common man?

4.5.5. Sociological research

Whenever possible, your voter targeting and analysis should be tested through solid sociological research. Campaigns that are not based on solid research are like drivers at night without headlights. They often do not see what is right in front of them until it is too late.

Most politicians everywhere believe that they have a natural gift for understanding "the people." They believe that they know, without doing research, what issues to discuss, what values to invoke, and what concerns to address in order to attract the interest of their voters. They are often surprised either by the results of a political poll or by the results on Election Day.

Most political activists use two types of sociological research to help them plan their campaign strategies: focus groups and political polling. Focus groups are designed to gain unscientific, qualitative knowledge about the values, attitudes and concerns of voters, while political polling is used to gain scientific, quantitative knowledge. The theory and methodology of sociological research is beyond the scope of this book; however there are some materials on polling included in Appendix D.

4.6.   Worksheet 3: Geographic Targeting

Answer the following questions to determine the geographic targeting for your campaign:

- ❖ Where do all the candidates live? Are there any distinct geographic areas of support for any particular candidate?
- ❖ What are the past performances of similar candidates in each area of the district?
- ❖ What is the level of Persuadability of voters in each area of the district?
- ❖ What is the expected turnout of each area of the district?

4.7.   Worksheet 4: Demographic Targeting

Answer the following questions to determine the demographic targeting for your campaign:

- ▪ What are the demographic profiles (age, gender, profession, education, etc.) of all the viable candidates, including your candidate?
- ▪ What demographic groups should support your candidate?
- ▪ Are there enough votes within these groups to win the election?
- ▪ Are there other candidates appealing to the same demographic groups?
- ▪ What demographic groups will you concede to your opponents?
- ▪ What collateral groups might you appeal to if need be?

4.8.   Worksheet 5: Bringing Together all the Targeting

Answer the following questions and incorporate the answers into your written campaign plan:

- ❖ List all the likely supporters, both geographically and demographically.

- ❖ List all the potential supporters, both geographically and demographically.
- ❖ List all the unlikely supporters that you will concede to your opponents.
- ❖ What are the values of both likely and potential supporters? Do they differ in any significant way?
- ❖ What are their attitudes?
- ❖ What issues concern these voters?
- ❖ What leadership qualities are they looking for?
- ❖ Which of the answers to questions 4 through 7 are likely to be the most important factors influencing your target voters in this election?

By targeting your voters before you begin your campaign and incorporating this targeting into every facet of your campaign plan, you will be able to stretch your resources much further than if you simply "go out and campaign." Your campaign will be able to maintain control by making sure that the only voters that you are spending time and money on are those voters that not only live in the ward, constituency, district or province and are registered to vote, but that are likely to vote for your candidate after hearing your message. The formula is straightforward: research, target, plan, contact and win.

National Democratic Institute for International Affairs (2009). Political Campaign Planning Manual, A step by step guide to winning elections, Washington, DC: NDI.

CHAPTER FIVE

STEP FOUR- DETERMINING AND DEVELOPING THE CAMPAIGN MESSAGE

5.1. What is a Message?

Messaging vary tremendously between campaigns. Once you have decided who your target audience is, you need to decide what you will say to persuade them to vote for you. This is your campaign message. It tells the voters why you are running for this particular office and why they should choose you over your opponents for the same office. Sounds simple, doesn't it? Well, once again, it is deceptively complicated.

For example, let us start off by saying what a message is not. A campaign message is not the candidate's program of what they will do if elected, it is not a list of the issues the candidate will address, and it is not a simple, catchy phrase or slogan. All of these things can be part of a campaign message, depending on whether or not they will persuade voters, but they should not be confused with the message, a simple statement that will be repeated over and over throughout the campaign to persuade your target voters.

In many cases, candidates are seeking office due to strong feelings on a single issue. However, if the voters do not share the candidate's strong feeling, the candidate needs to determine if he/she is comfortable focusing on other issues.

5.1.1. What voters care about and how they get their information

There are two important things you need to remember about voters. The first is what is important to them and the second is their sources of information.

Take a minute to think, what are the most important issues in the average voters' minds? Their list of priorities is probably something like the following:

- How are they getting along with their husband, wife, boyfriend, girlfriend or whatever?
- How are their children or parents doing, either in school or in life?
- How are they doing in their jobs or whether or not they will have enough money to get by?
- How their football team is doing, why do they keep losing and whether or not they will be able to see the next game?
- Who should they vote for in the election tomorrow?

The point is that you and your election campaign are pretty low in the average voter's list of priorities and rightly so. All of the other things higher on the list will have much more direct impact on their lives in the very short term and, with a little attention from them, they will have much more impact on those things.

The second thing to remember is that voters are being bombarded with information every day. They get news on television and the radio, they get reports at work, they get advertisements all the time, and they hear that juicy piece of gossip about the neighbor down the street. Candidates think that their competition is the other person running for the same office, when in reality their competition for the voter's attention is all the other sources of information the voter receive every day. Your campaign message has to break through that thick wall of other information.

So, while candidates and campaign workers are spending hours and hours, days and days, months and months, thinking about, worrying about, doing something about this campaign, voters will give you a minute or two of their precious time and attention. You must not waste it.

Advertising companies understand all this. That is why they come up with a clear, concise message and spend a lot of money making sure their target audience sees, hears and tastes that message as many times as possible. You must do the same thing. You can spend hours and hours writing the most thoughtful position papers and newsletter articles, but if the voters throw them away in 15 seconds, if no one reads them, you are wasting your time.

This said, you should have the greatest respect for voters. They can see through an insincere message quicker than the politician can say it.

5.2. Characteristics of a Good Message

There are a number of criteria that make up a strong message.

5.2.1. A message must be short

Voters have very little patience for listening to long-winded politicians. If you cannot effectively deliver your message to a voter in less than one minute, then you will surely lose that voter's attention and probably their vote.

5.2.2. A message must be truthful and credible

The message needs to come from the values, practices, policies and history of the candidate. It cannot be inconsistent with the candidate's background. In addition, your message should be believable; candidates who make unrealistic promises simply add to voter apathy. Voters must believe what you say, both about yourself and what you will do, is true. It is therefore critically important to back-up your statements with evidence of experience or knowledge from your personal past. Saying you understand a problem or issue without demonstrating why or how you understand it is a waste of your time and the voters' time.

5.2.3. A message must be persuasive and important to voters

You must talk about topics that are important to your target audience. These topics will often be problems that voters face every day in their lives, not issues that politicians think are important to public policy. Voters are more likely to support candidates that talk to them about their jobs, the children's education or their pension than a candidate that talks about the budget, even though the budget may deal with all of these things. Remember you are trying to convince the voter that you are the best candidate to represent them and persuade them to do something, namely vote for you.

5.2.4. A message must show contrast

Voters must make a choice between you and other candidates. You need to make it clear to the voters how you are different from the other candidates in the race by contrasting yourself with them. If every candidate stands for economic development and social security, then voters will have no way of making a clear choice. If, on the other hand, you support tax cuts for this particular industry and your opponents do not, then the voters will have a very clear choice. Filling out the message box, which will be discussed in some detail later, will help with developing a clear contrast. Appendix E also provides some advice on how to draw a clear contrast with your opponent.

5.2.5. A message must be clear and speak to the heart

Your message must be delivered in language the voters use and understand easily. Too often politicians want to impress the voters with how smart they are, using technical words that either the voters do not understand or have no real meaning for them. You do not want to make the voting public have to work to understand what you are talking about.

Creating a visual image in the minds of voters is much better. Talk about people, things and real life situations to describe abstract ideas, such as "economic policy."

Politics is an emotional business and politicians who appeal to the hearts of voters generally defeat those who appeal to their heads. This does not mean that you should abandon the intellectual basis of your party or candidacy or that you should underestimate the intelligence of the voter. This means that you must find a way to tie your campaign message to the core values of your voters and make it clear that you understand the problems they face every day.

5.2.6. A message must be targeted

As discussed in "Step Three: Targeting the Voters," if your campaign message speaks to everyone, then in reality, it speaks to no one. The people who will vote for you are different from those who will not vote for you and both groups have different concerns. Your campaign must determine what these differences are and address your message to your likely supporters. In many cases, voters just need clear information about who really represents their interests. If they have that information, they will vote for that person. Politicians often fail to provide that clear information. They seem to expect voters to either somehow know it without being told or wade through everything the politician says to figure it out.

5.2.7. A message must be repeated again and again

Once your campaign determines what message will persuade your target voters to vote for your candidate, then you must repeat that same message at every opportunity. Voters are not paying attention to your campaign. Just because you say something does not mean they are listening or will remember what you said. For your message to register with the voters, they have to hear the same message many times in many different ways. So, if you change your message, you are only confusing the voters.

5.3. Worksheet 6: Why are You Running for this Office?

❖ Make a list of all the reasons why voters should vote for your candidate or your party.

❖ Now, choosing the most compelling reasons from above, write a brief statement about your candidate. This should be the answer to the question "why are you running for this office?" or "why should I support you?"

❖ Now, read the statement aloud and time yourself. You must be able to complete the statement in less than one minute. If you go over a minute, you must trim your message. Takeout any long phrases or explanations. Remember that voters will not be paying attention to all of your ten-minute speech.

❖ Grade your message against the above criteria. Is it credible and truthful? Do you backup your statements with personal experience from your past? Are you talking about things that will be important to your target voters? If you are running over one minute, then there are probably a lot of useless words and phrases that you can delete. Do you offer a clear choice between your candidate and your major opponents?

❖ Now rewrite your statement, taking into account those things you missed the first time. You still must keep your message under one minute. As you write and rewrite this statement, as you begin using it as you talk to voters, it will continue to improve.

5.4. Worksheet 7: The Message Box

The American political strategist Paul Tully designed the following exercise to help candidates design their messages and think through their election strategies methodically and thoroughly. He called this exercise the "message box." The message box requires candidates not only to determine what they will be saying during the campaign, but also how they will respond to their opponents' attacks.

On a large piece of paper or a chalkboard, draw the following graph:

What We Say About Us	What We Say About Them
What They Say About Us	What They Say About Them

Now fill in each box with as much information as possible.

5.4.1. What we say about us

How do the candidate and the campaign define themselves? This quadrant is filled with all the positive things the campaign wants the voters to know about your candidate. This is mostly the information you put down in Worksheet 6.

5.4.2. What we say about them

How does your campaign define your various opponents? This quadrant is filled with all the negative things the campaign would want the voters to think about your opponents, the reasons why voters should not vote for them. You may not say these things directly, but you should at least know what they are.

5.4.3. What they say about us

In this quadrant the campaign must begin to view your candidate and campaign from the point of view of your major opponents. What would the opponents want the voters to think about your candidate and why, in their opinion, should the voters not vote for your candidate?

5.4.4. What they say about them

As you continue to view your campaign through the eyes of your major opponents, now look at how they would define themselves. Why, in your opponents' opinion, should voters vote for them?

If done correctly, the complete message box should outline everything that could possibly be said during the election campaign by both your candidate and all of your major opponents. This includes things that may go unsaid or charges made by implication. For example, if you say that you are the more experienced candidate, by implication you are saying your opponents lack experience. By saying you are honest; you can imply that your opponents are corrupt. Your opponents can do this to your candidate as well. If, for example, when they say that they care about education, they are implying that you do not care about education. How will you respond to their charges, both stated and implied?

Often the difficulty is putting yourself in the role of your opponents and view your opponents positively and yourself negatively. Remember, just because your opponents say it does not mean that it has to be true. The real question is what will voters believe? If you do not respond to what they say, the voters may take their information as the truth.

The other important part of this exercise is to have answers for the possible charges your opponents will say about you. If they attack you or blame you for something in one of their boxes, how do you respond in your boxes?

5.5. Credibility - Raising Your Credibility on Voters and Lowering Your Opponents Credibility on Voters

As you consider your message and develop the contrast with your opponents, you should keep in mind that what you want to accomplish in the end is to have more credibility with your target voters than you opponents have. In other words, you want more of your target voters to view you as the better candidate and vote for you. There are two ways to accomplish this.

First, you can do and say things to raise your credibility in the eyes of the voters. You may do this by concentrating on your positive characteristics and popular stands on issues.

Second, you can try to lower your opponents' credibility in the eyes of the voters. You may do this by pointing out what voters will view as the negative characteristics of your opponents or unpopular positions on issues.

Which of these methods you choose and in what combination most often depends on what position you find yourself in over the course of the campaign. Often, if you are ahead in the polls and can expect to win easily, then you can concentrate on raising your credibility. You will not want to mention your opponents and bring attention to them. You also do not want to risk alienating voters by running what may be viewed as a negative campaign or unnecessarily attacking your opponents.

On the other hand, if you find yourself behind in the polls, raising your credibility may not be enough to win. In this case you may want to raise your credibility and, at the same time, work to lower your opponents' credibility. In a sense, you have nothing to lose (you are already losing) by attacking your opponents and everything to gain (you may win).

5.6.   Issues and the Campaign Message

As stated above, your campaign message is not your program or the list of issues you will address. Still, your campaign should address the issues that are important to your target voters.

You may think of your campaign's message as the trunk of a large oak tree, strong, stable and well rooted in your candidate's values and personal experience. Following this analogy, the campaign issues that you will discuss are the tree branches, covering a wide area but all firmly connected to your message tree trunk. Similarly, your campaign must cover a broad range of issues that concern your target audience. However, in order to address these issues effectively, in order to avoid confusing your target voters with a jumble of incoherent program ideas, you must tie all of your issues to your campaign message.

Governor Bill Clinton's 1992 challenge campaign against President George Bush provides an excellent example of how to do this. Clinton's message was a simple one:

After twelve years of Republican leadership resulting in social stagnation and economic recession, the American people are ready for change. The choice in 1992 is clear: change or more of the same.

The Clinton campaign did an excellent job of tying each campaign issue to this message. If, for example, Bill Clinton talked about health care reform, the question was change or more of the same? If Clinton talked about education, the economy, social welfare or anything else, the question was always the same, change or more of the same?

It should be noted that the Clinton message strategy met all of the criteria for a good message and followed the recommendations outlined in this *Campaign Treatise Handbook.* For example:

The campaign message was based on solid research. Political polls and focus groups showed that the American people were, in fact, hungry for change.

The message was short, truthful and credible, important to a majority of voters, showed contrast with Bush and the Republicans, and spoke clearly to the heart of the American people.

The message was designed for a discrete target audience, workers and the middle class who felt that Republican policies were not helping them to get ahead.

Bill Clinton stayed on message continuously. He repeated the same message, "change or more of the same," at every opportunity.

5.7. Issue Selection

It is important not to confuse a problem with an issue. A problem is a condition that needs addressing, such as economic problems. An issue is a solution or partial solution to a problem, such as increased investment in education and small business to address problems with the economy.

As you consider what issues your campaign will address through its message, there are two important things to remember. First, how important is this particular issue to your target voters? Second, which candidate has the better position on this issue in the eyes of the voters? Too often, candidates either focus on issues that are not important to voters, ignoring more important issues, or they focus on issues where their opponents' can claim with a certain amount of credibility or a better position on the issue. The following exercise illustrates this point.

5.8. Worksheet 8: Determining Issue Importance and Position

Suppose that your candidate is considering ten issues that may become factors in the upcoming election campaign. In order to preserve the focus of your campaign, you want to concentrate on only two or three, but which ones? Using this type of graph may help you choose.

First, rank the ten issues (A through J) in order of importance to your target voters (the numbers along the side of the box). In this example, Issue C is most important to voters, followed by Issues G, F, J, E, A, D, H, B, and I respectively.

Second, rank the issues in order of how well your candidate does on these issues in comparison to your major opponents (the numbers along the bottom of the box). In this example, the voters believe the candidate will best be able to address issue G, followed by Issues J, A, I, B, E, H, F, C and D respectively.

Issues	Importance	Position
A	5	8
B	2	6
C	10	2
D	4	1
E	6	5
F	8	3
G	9	10
H	3	4
I	1	7
J	7	9

Source: National Democratic Institute for International Affairs (2009).

Now, plot out these ten issues as shown on the graph, placing them in the various quadrants. The example should look something like the following graph:

Very Important/Poor Position	Very Important/Good Position
10 C	
9	G
8 F	
7	J
6 E	
5	A
4 D	
3 H	
2	B
1	I
0 1 2 3 4 5	6 7 8 9 10
Less Important/Poor Position	Less Important/Good Position

Source: National Democratic Institute for International Affairs (2009).

Your campaign should focus on the issues that fall into the upper-right-hand quadrant. In this example, the candidate should focus on Issues G and J. The target audience believes that these issues are important and they believe that your candidate is best positioned to deal with them.

Focusing on issues in the lower-right-hand quadrant (Less Important/Good Position) will not help your candidate very much because the target audience does not consider them very important. Although focusing on these issues will not hurt the candidate, you should not waste scarce resources talking about things that the target audience does not care about.

Focusing on issues in the upper left-hand quadrant (Very Important/Poor Position) is actually quite dangerous. Although the target audience considers them important, they believe that other candidates are more likely to better deal with them. Thus, every time that your candidate talks about Issues C and F, your campaign is bringing the voters' attention to the strengths of your opponent. In other words, you are spending your own resources to help your opponent.

Candidates often wrongly believe that it is possible to change voter's minds about their positioning on issues. From a psychological standpoint, it is very difficult to change a voter's mind about any issue; it is much easier to turn the focus of the debate onto issues where your candidate is well positioned. In the example above, why should your candidate spend scarce resources trying to change people's minds about Issue C when he can immediately get favorable attention talking about Issue G?

5.9. Sociological Research and Message Development

Your campaign's message development, like its voter targeting and analysis, should be based on solid research. For example, when you fill out an issue chart, like the one above, you should not sit and guess about the relative importance of each issue and your position on it. If at all possible, your rankings should come from polling information.

Also, you should use sociological research to test your campaign's message before the start of the election campaign. You would never spend thousands or millions on a car without driving it to see whether or not it runs. Why would you spend the same thousands of dollars to publicize a message without testing it to see whether or not it will be effective? Focus groups may provide the best low-cost alternative to polling for testing your campaign's message.

5.10. Stay on Message

Once you have developed a clear, concise, persuadable message it is important that you use that message at every opportunity and not deviate from it throughout the campaign. This is called "staying on message."

In the next chapter, various methods of contacting voters will be discussed. It is important that every method you use incorporates the same message. Often one type of voter contact will reinforce the message delivered using a different type of voter contact. For example, a brief thirty second television commercial can reinforce the message delivered in the literature and in the press. By using the same message in all your voter contact, you are less likely to confuse voters who may not be paying close attention and reinforce what they have heard. It is often said that voters have to hear the same message as many as seven times for it to sink in and register with them.

Often the opposition or the press will do something or say something that will drag you and the campaign "off message." If you respond, you will not be talking about the issues you want to talk about but will be talking about the issues your opponent wants to talk about. In most cases, you should respond to any charges but then quickly shift the conversation back to the issues and the message you want to address.

It is also important that you do not bury the message under too much information. After talking to supporters, candidates and political activists often wrongly believe that voters want more information. One should not confuse ordinary voters who may still need to be persuaded with supporters who are probably already convinced to vote for your candidate or party and want more information. You can often supply this need for more information in the form of position papers or articles but you must summarize the main points in a one page press release that delivers the message in the first sentence. You should further summarize the message in a quality piece of literature that grabs the voters' attention with pictures and headlines and doesn't let go until your message is delivered. This literature will be the bulk of your voter contact delivery method. If someone says that they want more information you can give them the press release or position paper. How to create quality literature will be discussed in some length, but the point is to deliver your message as effectively as possible to as many voters in your target audience as possible.

National Democratic Institute for International Affairs (2009). Political Campaign Planning Manual, A step by step guide to winning elections, Washington, DC: NDI.

CHAPTER SIX

STEP FIVE- DEVELOPING A VOTER CONTACT PLAN

6.1. A Voter Contact Plan

Do not waste precious resources trying to contact everyone in your ward, constituency or district. Once you have decided whom you will be talking to and what you will be saying, the next step is to decide how you will be saying it. In other words, how will you get your campaign's message out to voters?

Before you look at the various methods for reaching voters, there are some important points that apply to all of the methods. First is the rule of finite resources, which means that you must determine how much each method will cost in terms of time, money and people. Second is the interchangeability of the resources and the methods; meaning that you can often accomplish the same task using different resources. Finally, there is the effectiveness of each method at persuading voters, identifying supporters and turning out your vote. It is important to plan well in advance for each phase of the campaign, including turning voters out on Election Day.

6.2. The Rule of Finite Resources

As stated before, a political campaign is a communication process and all campaigns have three basic resources available to accomplish this communication - time, money and people. These resources can come together in an unlimited number of combinations and the trick is to select the best possible combination and use all three resources in the most efficient manner. You want to make the largest impact on the voters for each volunteer hour and each amount of money you spend.

In planning the voter contact part of your campaign, it is critically important to remember that you have finite resources. Every decision to do something is a decision not to do something else. When you have twenty volunteers, hand out literature, and these twenty volunteers cannot make phone calls at the same time. When you spend money on television, you do not have that money to spend on mail. Time spent greeting shoppers at the market are time taken from going door to door. It is important to budget all three resources - time, money and people - so that you have them when you need them and all three resources are used most efficiently. You want to make the largest impact on the voters while using as few of these resources as possible.

6.3. Interchangeability of Resources and Methods

It is important to remember that you can often use different resources and different methods to accomplish the same objective. Suppose you decide that you need to persuade 10,000 voters to vote for you. One thousand reliable volunteers can go door to door tomorrow and persuade 10 voters each to vote for your candidate (no time, no money but lots of people). By yourself, you can personally talk to 10,000 voters, at 50 voters a day over the next 200 days (no money, no people but lots of time). Or you can contact all 10,000 tomorrow without any help by airing a great television commercial. It will cost you a lot of money (no people, any time but money).

These are extreme examples, but they illustrate how interchangeable the resources and the methods are. You need to first figure out what you want to accomplish and then figure out which of the many ways is best for you to achieve your objective. If one method does not seem possible, you can often find another method. This is why planning is absolutely necessary. It is the campaign that does not have a written plan which often finds that it cannot raise the money it needs, does not have the volunteers it needs and has squandered its time.

6.4. Effectiveness of Your Voter Contact

Each type of voter contact can accomplish three things to varying degrees - persuade target voters, identify supporters and turnout your vote. These varying degrees determine the effectiveness of your voter contact effort. It is important that a campaign choose methods that, when combined; accomplish all three of these tasks.

Now that you have a *clear, concise and effective message*, it is important to use that message to persuade your target group of voters that your candidate is the best choice. Voters need to know what your message is and they need to hear it many times for it to register with them. You must repeatedly communicate a persuasive message to people who will vote.

Finally, as the election period draws to a close, there comes a time when you can no longer persuade voters and your efforts should be spent on making sure that those people who support your candidate turnout to vote for your candidate.

In order to do this, you must have some way of identifying who supports you and who has been persuaded through your voter contact effort to support you. Well before Election Day you must have spent time identifying your supporters. It is also important to know how you will reach them in a very short period of time.

6.4.1. Persuade target voters

Most of your campaign effort will go toward persuading your target voters that you are the best candidate and it is in their interest to go to the polls and vote for you. Everything you have done up to this point - all the research, setting the goal, targeting the audience and developing a persuasive message - has brought you to this point. Now you need to decide what the easiest way for you to communicate with this large group of people and convince them to vote for you. There is no point in having a great message if the voters do not know about it.

People are often persuaded when they hear the same thing from many different sources. If they hear that you are a good candidate from a respected civic organization, meet the candidate going door to door, see some persuasive campaign literature, and read a favorable article in the newspaper, then they will more likely remember the candidate and more likely vote for that candidate. None of these contacts should be left to chance. A well organized campaign will make sure that all of these contacts happen and that the same message is delivered each time so that the message reinforces itself each time.

6.4.2. Get out the vote

It does no good to have spent months persuading your target audience that you are the best candidate if they do not go to the polls on Election Day and vote for you. Individual voters often feel that their one single vote does not matter. They need to know that they are part of something bigger and that their support for your candidate is important. Often a simple reminder - either a phone call or piece of literature - can be enough to ensure that they vote.

The **"get out the vote" (GOTV)** effort is often viewed as a separate phase of the campaign. In fact, it should be viewed as the final phase toward which everything else in the campaign builds. If you compare a political campaign to a business selling a product, in this case selling the candidate to the voters, then Election Day is the only day in which you can make the sale. It is important that the voters be motivated enough to "buy your product" on that one day. The deadline for all the campaign and particularly the GOTV part of the campaign is the close of the polls on Election Day. Either you are prepared to make that final push or you are not. There are no second chances.

This GOTV effort can be accomplished in many different ways but the various methods differ in one important factor - whether or not the campaign knows who is being contacted.

In areas where a candidate has considerable support - say six out of every ten voters will vote for them - it is not necessary to identify supporters. You will know that the more voters you remind about Election Day and make sure that they vote; that your candidate will receive the majority of the votes. In these areas you can organize what is called a "blind pull" of voters or pulling everyone to the polls regardless of whether or not you know whom they are supporting. In these areas where the support is very strong the campaign can put up signs reminding voters about Election Day and encouraging them to vote. They may want to phone as many of the voters as possible to make sure they turn out.

In other areas where support is less sure, you will want to only remind those voters you know to support you. It is therefore important to have spent time identifying which voters will support you well in advance of the GOTV effort. Once you have developed a database or list of supporters, it is important to have the resources and the means of communicating with them in the short period of time just before the election. It is therefore important to budget enough time, money and people and have a realistic plan of how you will get in touch with your supporters.

6.4.3. Voter identification

Because so much of the GOTV effort relies on having an accurate list of supporters well in advance of Election Day, it is important to know how you will identify supporters starting early in the campaign. You need to spend resources persuading your voters. However, if you only communicate with them, you are relying on them to go to the polls on their own. This can be a gamble that you need not take. You can increase your chances if you know who has been convinced and you have the ability to get them to the polls.

It is often possible to find out which candidate voters support just by asking them. People generally like to be asked their opinion and are willing to tell you what they are thinking. Develop a simple "1-2-3" scale so that a confirmed supporter is labeled a "1," an undecided voter is a "2," and a supporter of an opponent is a "3." As your campaign communicates with voters, try to judge their level of support. You will want to spend most of your resources on number "2" voters in your target audience.

As you identify voters, you will want to have some method of keeping track of them and their levels of support. You can use a simple card file or even better, a computer database that you will be able to continuously update and sort the files to meet your needs.

It is important that this database be as accurate as possible. Do not consider someone a supporter unless they have told you so directly. Often people will not want to offend you or argue with you if they have not made up their mind or actually support your opponent. For this reason you may not want to bias them by telling them you are calling from the campaign.

6.5. Types of Voter Contact Activities

With all of these things in mind, it is important to ask the following questions as you consider the various types of voters contact.

- ❖ How much does it cost in time, money and people?
- ❖ Do you know what voters are being reached?
- ❖ Are they being persuaded?
- ❖ Can you find out if they support your candidate and make sure that they vote for your candidate?

Each of the following types of voter contact meets these various criteria to varying degrees.

6.5.1. Literature drop

A literature drop is when volunteers go door-to-door leaving a piece of literature about the candidate at each household. A large number of volunteers can cover a large area relatively quickly and, because you know that the houses are in the voting district, you know that only potential voters are being reached. The volunteers are not talking with voters, so they do not identify supporters, but they can leave a reminder to vote at the supporters' homes just before Election Day.

6.5.2. Literature handouts

Your campaign can also hand out literature wherever people gather in large numbers. This could be at markets, factory gates, church, bars, train stations, motor parks, metro stops, etc. While this may be a lot easier or quicker than the literature drop at the voters' homes, it is less targeted because you are not certain that the people who take your literature live in the area or can vote for your candidate.

Often this type of activity is targeted around a particular issue that will concern those gathered in that area. For example, you may want to hand out a piece of literature about saving a factory at the gates of the factory, or repairing the metro at a metro stop, or building a new senior center where seniors are gathered.

6.5.3. Mail

Sending campaign literature to voters through the mail can be very effective at delivering your message and persuading them to vote for you. Depending on what type of list you have, you may be able to target voters either by geography or demographics (age, gender, etc.). For example, you could send something outlining your stand on one issue to senior citizens and send a different piece outlining your stand on a different issue to young women. Again, you will know that those who receive your mail live in the district.

6.5.4. Door to door

One of the most effective ways to persuade voters is to go from house to house, apartment to apartment, door to door, talking to individual voters one at a time. You are able to hear the problems they face, tailor your message to meet their individual concerns and gage the level of support. Often voters are impressed that a candidate would bother to come meet them and you can gain their support just by making the effort.

Obviously this is going to be very time consuming method of voter contact. Depending on the types of neighborhoods you will be walking in, a candidate who is disciplined can talk to approximately 50 voters a night or around 300 voters a week. This is assuming that you canvass for about three hours a night and spend no more than three minutes with each voter (allowing a little bit of time to get from door to door). Now you understand why you have to be able to deliver your message in less than a minute.

Because door to door is so time consuming, there are a number of things you can do to make it more effective and make sure you stay on schedule. Once again, these things require forethought and planning. You may consider adapting these methods to fit your circumstances.

Voters are more likely to remember a candidate's message if they hear it more than once, so a candidate is more likely to make an impression if they can increase their voter contact at the door from one time to two, three or four times. This can be done by first having the campaign deliver a piece of literature to the target voters' homes a week before the candidate walks the neighborhood, stating that the candidate will be walking. This can be either mailed or dropped by volunteers and should deliver the campaign message.

Then, when the candidate actually shows up, they are keeping their first promise to voters.

The candidate then walks the neighborhood delivering the message both verbally and through a piece of literature that is left with the voter. Finally, if the campaign is able to keep track of who the candidate talked to and who was missed, it will be able to deliver a follow-up card a week later, stating that the candidate was either happy to have met the voter or sorry to have missed them.

The best way to keep the canvass on schedule is to have a trusted volunteer accompany the candidate as they go door to door. This person is responsible for carrying all the literature, knocking on the doors, and introducing the candidate when someone answers the door. The volunteer then moves on to the next door while the candidate talks to the voter, keeping a record of which doors answered and which not. If the candidate gets bogged down with a voter who wants to talk, it is the volunteer's role to go back and tell the candidate and the voter that they have to keep moving. In this way it is the volunteer who plays the role of the bad guy.

6.5.5. Phoning

The telephone can be used to persuade voters to vote for your candidate, identify supporters and remind those supporters to go vote for your candidate. Each of these should be a separate phone call. Most often the phone is used to identify supporters and turnout the vote. Both of these can be relatively short calls.

Phone calls can be made either from volunteers' homes or from a central location with a lot of phones. These central locations, called *phone banks*, can be either businesses or organizations with a lot of separate phone lines already in place, that allow the campaign to use them after hours to call voters. They can also be extra phone lines put into the headquarters for just this purpose.

Either way, phone banks have a number of advantages over having volunteers make the calls from their homes. First, the campaign can supervise the phone calls at a phone bank and make sure that the calls are being made. Second, the volunteers gain support from other volunteers making the calls. It is often important to share the experience, either good or bad, of the last phone call. Finally, the campaign has immediate control over the process, can deal with problems immediately, answer questions and receive instant feedback.

Sometimes the script the volunteers are using when they talk to voters does not work and must be changed. Or sometimes the campaign may want to shift from phoning one district to another quickly. This can be more easily done at a phone bank.

In both a phone bank and having volunteers call from home, it is important to have clear written instructions for the volunteers including the purpose of making the calls and an easy to follow script of what to say on the phone when talking to voters. It may also be important to explain what not to do, such as argue with voters. Volunteers should understand that it is important to make as many calls as possible, as quickly as possible and that arguing with voters will only slow them down and is unlikely to change the voter's mind.

Often when identifying voters that support a candidate, it is helpful if the campaign does not identify itself. The voters will be much more likely to give a truthful answer if they believe it is a poll rather than the campaign calling.

Sample scripts are provided in Appendix F.

6.5.6. Visibility

Visibility is anything the campaign does to catch the voters' eye. This can be billboards by the side of the road, signs at supporters houses, posters on poles, stickers on cars, volunteers or the candidate waving to traffic, car caravans with decorated cars driving through key neighborhoods, the candidates name on tee-shirts, coffee mugs, caps etc. While this may raise the voter awareness about the campaign and the name recognition of the candidate, it can only reinforce the campaign message. It is a very poor method of persuading voters. It also reaches a broad audience rather than a targeted audience. People who live outside the area or otherwise cannot or will not vote for the candidate will see the signs. Finally, there is no way of identifying who is supporting your candidate. However this method can be used very effectively to remind voters in strong support areas to go vote.

6.5.7. Endorsements

The candidate can meet with various opinion leaders in an attempt to persuade them to support the campaign. These opinion leaders can be newspaper editorial boards or representatives of issue oriented or community based organizations. The effectiveness at reaching voters depends on the influence these leaders or their organizations have on the voters. Time is often spent winning this support early in the campaign when voters aren't paying attention to the election but the opinion leaders are.

6.5.8. Coffees

A "coffee" is the term used to describe small meetings in the homes of supporters where they invite friends to meet the candidate. These have the advantage of face-to-face contact with the candidate, the most persuasive form of voter contact. They can also be used for volunteer recruitment and small donor fundraising. They tend to be labor and time intensive. A good coffee program can be very difficult to organize.

If the campaign decides to organize a coffee program as part of its direct voter contact, there should be one person responsible for finding volunteers who are willing to host the coffees and making all the arrangements. A good program will have at least one coffee per night and often two or three coffees scheduled per night. The candidate can stop in, meet the voters, and say a few words and move on to the next event. As with door to door, it is important that the candidate meet as many voters as possible and the campaign should keep a record of those who attend the coffees. In this case the multiple communications take the form of an invitation, which states the campaign message, literature and a few words by the candidate at the event, and a thank you to those who attended following the event. Because the invitations also deliver the message, you should not hesitate to send out as many as possible. Only those voters who actually know the host will probably show up.

The campaign should consider organizing at least one or two coffees per targeted area.

6.5.9. Friends of a friend

A "friends" program is when supporters and volunteers in the campaign personally contact people they know and ask them to vote for the candidate. This can be done by having them send a pre-made card to people who live near them or by having them, call people they know in the area. It is important that the campaign keep track of who will be making this type of effort on behalf of the campaign and who will be contacted. Organization is the key. Because this contact is often made just before Election Day, this is often considered part of the "get out the vote" effort.

6.5.10. Preset events

Preset events are events set up by people or organizations outside the campaign where candidates or their representatives are able to meet voters. These can be as diverse as debates sponsored by outside groups or parades that allow all the candidates to participate. The effectiveness as a voter contact method depends on the audience reached. Because these types of events may offer little feedback from the voters, the importance can often be gauged in the amount of press it will receive.

6.5.11. Created events

The campaign can also create events to gain exposure. These may be rallies to motivate supporters or press conferences to highlight the campaigns stand on an issue. Again, the effectiveness for voter contact is often gauged in the amount of press the event will receive. The advantage of created events is that the campaign can control the situation and often deliver a clear message. The disadvantage is that created events often take up a lot of time, money and people to organize. You must make sure that the message is persuasive and reaches enough of the targeted audience to be effective.

6.5.12. Earned media - the press

Politics and elections are such rare and important events (relatively speaking), that they actually receive considerably more press than many other events in the same area (most candidates do not believe this). Furthermore, because the press is a source of information outside the campaign, voters often respect it. Still, the press has its own agenda and many demands on its time and resources. If you use newspapers, television, and radio to get your campaign message out, you need good relations with the reporters, a compelling reason for them to tell your story, as well as an easily understood point to your message. Many campaigns have a press secretary and separate press operations just to deal with all of this. Still, remember that this is just another form of voter contact and should be coordinated with your other forms of voter contact.

The nature of the district and its media outlets will determine the importance of media relations in your district. However, generally speaking it is essential that your campaign establish good relationships with print and broadcast journalists in your region for two reasons.

First, the mass media (relatively speaking) is free of cost for the campaign. Every time a journalist prints or broadcasts a story about your campaign, you have the opportunity to get your message out to your target audience at no direct money cost to your campaign.

Second, the mass media is often considered credible. Voters are much more likely to believe positive information about your candidate if it comes from an "independent" source (the mass media) than if it comes from a "biased" source (your campaign).

If you decide that you want to use the press to communicate and persuade voters, then it is important to have a plan as to how you will accomplish this. Many campaigns have a press secretary who is responsible for developing this strategy, building a relationship with the press and communicating the message to the press. One of the press secretary's first tasks is to develop a comprehensive list of all the media outlets in the area, complete with reporters' names, phone numbers, emails and deadlines.

It is important that you make the job of writing about the campaign as easy as possible for the reporters. Write press releases in the style of a news story, as you would want them to write it. Provide as much backup data and sources (complete with phone numbers) as you possibly can. At the same time, make sure that everything is clear and reinforces your message. You do not want to make it too difficult for the reporter to figure out what you are saying. If you provide a position paper, provide them with a press release that summarizes your position in one page.

Press conferences should be well scripted and be important enough that it is worth the time of the press to come to them. Provide a press packet with a photo of the candidate, their biography, any campaign literature, relevant position papers, press clippings, and press releases. It is important that every communication with the press reinforces your overall campaign strategy. If the press wants to discuss something other than your message - for example, your opponent's message, answer their questions as quickly as possible and finish by restating your message. It is often the job of the press secretary to know what the press will ask before they ask it so that the candidate is not blind-sided by a reporter's question.

All of this is hard work and often takes time. This is called earned media because you have to work for it.

The process by which journalists and editors decide what articles to print, or what stories to broadcast can vary greatly. Thus, you must modify your press strategy to fit the realities of your area.

Nevertheless, those with broad experience of working with media have identified several rules that your campaign should take into account:

- A very short election cycle will make the mass media absolutely crucial. Unless your campaign has unlimited financial resources, you will need the assistance of the mass media to get your message out in the short period of time allowed for campaigning.

- Press relations are often a full-time job. Every medium to large campaign must have a person whose only concern is getting publicity for the candidate. Even in smaller campaigns, this job should go to the campaign manager or assistant. The candidate cannot be his or her own press secretary.

- All candidates must stay "on message" at all times. Your candidate will have very few opportunities to appear on television or radio, or to be quoted in the newspaper. These precious opportunities must not be wasted talking about things that your target audience does not care about. Once you have taken the time to develop a campaign message, stick to that message relentlessly.

- All candidates should undergo some form of media training or preparation. Again, television and radio appearances are rare and precious. Do not waste them by being unprepared. Before any television or radio appearance, know exactly what you will say and practice it.

6.5.13. Paid media - television, radio and newspaper advertisements

Unfortunately, you will not be able to count on journalists to provide you with all the publicity you will need for your campaign. You may need to purchase additional publicity in the forms of newspaper, radio or television advertisements.

This is a less targeted way to reach voters than canvassing the area or sending direct mail because, while you reach a broad audience, again it is not clear that everyone who hears or sees your advertisement is able to vote for you or is in your target audience. Still, this can be a very persuasive form of communication with voters, particularly television. It is particularly good at reinforcing a message that is delivered in person, such as door to door.

6.5.14. Internet web pages

The most recent addition to the list of voter contact methods is placing a web page on the Internet. It should be remembered that the Internet is a passive form of communication, meaning that it does not go to the voters; the voters have to come to it. So, while you may be able to get some press from introducing your web site and while it can be an inexpensive way to convey a lot of information to those who are interested, it is not effective at reaching a particular, targeted audience (unless you are going for the nerd vote).

6.5.15. Combining various methods

Different campaigns at different levels will use different combinations of voter contact to reach voters. National political campaigns, which have to reach millions of voters, cannot afford the time of going door to door. They may use a combination of earned media and television advertisements to get the message out. On the other hand, small local campaigns may not be able to afford the amount of money television would cost to reach a small number of voters. Here it might make sense to have the candidate go door-to-door talking to voters, combined with a direct mail campaign to convey the same message to the same voters again. Following a direct mail program, a campaign with many volunteers may want to set up phone banks to call all the potential voters to identify who supports the candidate and who has been persuaded by the candidate's message.

With the varying resources of time, money and people, the combination of voter contact methods that can be combined is unlimited and no two campaigns will ever be alike. This is why it is vitally important to take all the data possible on the area, the voters, and all the candidates, and then the campaign must develop a workable, written plan to deliver the message.

6.6. Worksheet 9: Determining Which Voter Contact Methods to Use

Use the following chart to help determine which voter contact method your campaign will choose. It is important to be realistic. No campaign should consider using all of the methods listed. This would just spread your resources too thin and insure that you did none of them well. You will want to consider realistically what resources of time, money and people you will have available to you and how much each method will cost. It is also important to pick various methods that, when combined, will accomplish all of the tasks - persuading voters, identifying supporters and turning out your vote.

Make a list of all the methods you have decided to use in your campaign and try to determine in hard numbers how much time, money and people you will need to accomplish your objective.

	Effectiveness			Resources		
Voter contact task	Persuade Voters	Identify Supporters	Turn-out Vote	Time	Money	**People**
Literature Drop	Yes	No	Yes	Yes		**Yes**
Literature Handouts	Maybe	No	Maybe	Yes		
Mail	Yes	No	Yes		Yes	
Door to Door	Yes	Yes	No	Yes		**Yes**
Phoning	Maybe	Yes	Yes	Yes	Yes	**Yes**
Visibility	No	No	Yes	Yes	Yes	**Yes**
Endorsements	Yes	Maybe	Maybe	Yes		**Yes**
Coffees	Yes	Yes	No	Yes		**Yes**
Dear Friend	Yes	No	Yes	Yes		**Yes**
Preset Events	Maybe	Maybe	No	Yes		**Yes**
Created Events	Maybe	No	Maybe	Yes	Yes	**Yes**
Press	Yes	No	Maybe	Yes		
Advertisements	Yes	No	Yes		Yes	
Web Pages	**No**	**No**	**No**			

Source: National Democratic Institute for International Affairs (2009).

6.7. Creating Campaign Literature

Many of the methods of voter contact rely on quality campaign literature to deliver the message. It is therefore important that your literature be as effective as possible at delivering this message. When creating literature for a political campaign you must remember that most voters will not read it as carefully as you will or as you would like them to. It is important that you make it easy for the voters to understand your message in the short time that it takes them to decide to throw the literature away.

It is therefore important to quickly get the voters' attention and just as quickly convey your message. In other words, you need to keep your campaign literature simple and make it dramatic. You should tell a story about who your candidate is and why voters should vote for your candidate. Any other information you provide should back up the original message. There are a few techniques that can be used to grab the voter's attention and quickly deliver a message.

6.7.1. Single topic

In order to keep the message simple and make sure that it is grasped quickly, it is important that you do not try to convey any more than one idea in a piece of literature. For example, one piece of literature may tell how the candidate will fight crime or what the candidate will do to improve the economy but both topics should not be covered in the same piece of literature. The exception to this technique is "palm card" or general piece of campaign literature used to introduce the candidate. Here the theme is why voters should support the candidate and may include very brief statements on where the candidate stands on various issues.

6.7.2. Action photos

Too often campaign literature only has a portrait photo of the candidate. This does not tell the voter anything about the candidate and is a complete waste of space. Photos should show the candidate talking to someone or doing something.

Other action photos can both grab the voter's attention and convey a message quicker than words. For example, a picture of someone breaking into a building or pointing a gun on the cover of piece of literature dealing with crime will mean that voters are more likely to open it to see what it is about. The inside photo should show the candidate talking to police, thereby making the connection between the issue and the candidate. Pictures of children in school can help convey an education message, and pictures of closed businesses or people begging on the streets can convey a message of economic problems that will be addressed. Remember that these photos should convey action. Portraits of the candidate do not convey any information about who they are. Also, all photos can be black and white. Using color photos is too expensive and does not necessarily improve on the message conveyed.

6.7.3. Headlines

After looking at the photos, people will next read the headlines. The whole message should be understood in the headlines, a brief statement or two in large type. Everything else in the piece of literature will only reinforce this brief message. Too often the headlines are only headings and the voter is expected to read on to understand the point. Therefore it is important not to waste the headlines with headings such as "my program" or with useless statements that do not say anything such as "dear voter" or "vote."

6.7.4. Bulleted points

When listing a program, a biography or any other series of information, bullet the text rather than put it in paragraph forms. This makes it clear that there are five reasons to support the candidate or six things the candidate will do to improve the economy. These bullets can have headlines as well but the headlines should use action words such as "fighting crime" or "improving your economy."

6.7.5. Be specific

Without making promises that cannot be kept, it is important to be as specific as possible in offering solutions to the problems people face. The candidate "supports legislation that will..." does not mean that the legislation has to pass or accomplish the goal but it still conveys a stand on an issue.

6.7.6. Brevity

In campaign literature, less is more. Say whatever you want to say in as few words as possible. Between one hundred and three hundred words total should be the maximum in a single piece of literature. Remember that voters will not read long text because it requires more effort than they are willing to spend on something that does not immediately affect them. With this in mind, statements like "dear voter" can be eliminated because voters know that when they get a piece of literature they are the ones being addressed. These phrases are extra, unneeded words.

6.7.7. Common language

Use language that simply and clearly states what you want to get across. It is less important to impress voters with big words than it is to get your message across in language all voters will understand. In an election campaign, you do not have enough time nor is it your role to educate voters.

6.7.8. Stay on message

All campaign literature, no matter what the issue being discussed, should stick to the basic theme of the campaign. It is important that the same message be reinforced over and over, no matter what the issue. The campaign may even want to use the same phrases or slogans on all the literature to bring the point home to voters.

National Democratic Institute for International Affairs (2009). Political Campaign Planning Manual, A step by step guide to winning elections, Washington, DC: NDI.

CHAPTER SEVEN

——————————————————

STEP SIX- SECURITY

7.1.   Security Management Plan

The security plan of a candidate cuts across adequate security for the candidate, campaign team and ground, campaign office(s), Election Day security (this has become source of manipulation and systematic rigging) and collaboration with civil society groups, security agents and coordinating government agencies.

In any election, authorities take steps to ensure that voters, candidates, poll workers, observers, and other actors involved in an election experience the process free from fear or harm and to ensure that sensitive election materials are kept safe.

The specific security requirements for a given election will vary greatly depending on the context or environment. In places with enduring conflict, or where there is a significant potential for violence, securing an election will need to address a variety of factors and will likely involve deploying relatively large numbers of security personnel, such as police, allied forces or military forces, to protect physical locations, individuals and election materials. There should be plans in place for the secure transfer and storage of election materials, especially ballots and ballot boxes. Safeguards to any technologies used in the election process should also be adopted to prevent hacking, manipulation or rigging.

Potentials for violence in election periods come from political, economic and social dimensions of a society. Effective violence mitigation plans should often include identifying early warning signs, mobilizing citizen monitoring and mitigation efforts, dispatching properly trained security forces, coordinating among government agencies and educating the public, among other things. Multiple institutions, including Electoral Monitoring Bodies (EMBs), ministries of interior and other relevant bodies, may be involved in creating a secure election environment. Civil society, through Civil Society Organizations (CSOs), trade unions, religious and traditional institutions and leaders, and the media, also play important roles in creating a secure electoral environment by mediating, building intolerance for violence and enhancing public confidence in experiencing secure and sufficient electoral participation. In many countries, like Nigeria and Ghana, plans for electoral security take into account such activities by civil society.

7.2.   Tackling Electoral Violence

Electoral violence is violence intended to influence the electoral conduct of voters, candidates, officials, or other actors and/or to affect the electoral outcome. Electoral violence involves any use of force with the intent to cause harm or the threat to use force to harm persons or property involved in the electoral process. Typically, electoral violence happens among or even within the camps of electoral competitors in depraved and desperate efforts to gain office through elections. Sometimes, forces opposed to democratic governance may attack electoral targets to advance their quest for power outside of electoral competition.

Additional, violence, based on personal animosities or grievances between population groups, may take place in an election period though it is not directly related to elections. Election security planning has to consider the potentials for all of these types of violence and how to prevent, mitigate or end them while respecting fundamental human rights. Election violence as a vital tool to election riggers should be carefully checked as this has evolved into a systematic rigging means/process, more especially in developing countries.

7.3.   Significance of Election Security

In order for an election to be inclusive, free and fair, participatory, competitive and ultimately, to reflect the will of the people; it is essential that electoral candidates can campaign; citizens can cast informed, secret ballots without fear of retribution; officials can effectively administer the process; and civil society, media and parties can engage and observe, free from fear and harm. In many places, EMBs help coordinate processes and personnel to protect various aspects of elections. The candidate through the party should ensure that security plan for a given election takes into account the implications of deploying armed personnel. While their deployment can be necessary where potentials for electoral violence are significant, their presence may intimidate or dissuade citizens from participating and such area could be a candidate's winning zone (this is also a way of systematic rigging). Input from civil society in the planning phases can help ensure that citizens' concerns are more fully considered and are informed about the measures in place to ensure their security. At the same time, electoral security requires more comprehensive measures than deployment of security forces.

The analysis of past incidents and patterns of violence is vital for allocating anti-violence resources. Identifying early warning signs or indicators are necessary for preventative measures, while addressing rumors concerning potential or actual incidents of electoral violence is essential for mitigating potentials for violent reactions. Often, this means that information must be available in near real-time to be used effectively.

The physical security of election materials is also critical. If sensitive materials -- especially ballot papers, ballot boxes and results sheets- are not effectively and adequately secured, there is the potential for actual or perceived manipulation, diminishing public trust in the process and acceptance of the outcomes or results.

The public and electoral candidates must be informed of this aspect of electoral security to have confidence in the integrity of elections. The institutions involved in the security framework should be, and be seen to be transparent and unbiased. Information about election security measures can bolster citizens' trust in the process and enable full participation as voters, candidates, poll workers, observers, or other roles. Civil society and candidates/ contestants can examine the security measures in place to determine any necessary reforms going forward. With access to information about the election security apparatus and decision-making process, civil society, political parties, and media can make sure that the EMB and/or the security forces are following proper procedures and playing a positive role.

7.4.   **Worksheet 10: Security Plan Checklist**

List the entire security plan from campaign to Election Day, to results declaration of the winner(s).

- ❖ Why does election security matter?
- ❖ Define your security goal and appoint security Director
- ❖ Provide security for the candidate and family
- ❖ Ensure security for the campaign team, entourage and ground
- ❖ Avoiding security breaches by the campaign organization or team
- ❖ Work according to electoral rules and laws
- ❖ Quick and timely report any suspected breaches in electoral law(s) by the rival candidate, opponent or party. Possibly file a motion or litigation before the election date
- ❖ Assess social risk factors when contesting for national election or position.

CHAPTER EIGHT

STEP SEVEN: MAKING THE GOAL HAPPEN

8.1. Making it Happen

You have done the research, set the goal, targeted the audience, developed the message and figured out how you are going to deliver the message. You have also started to figure out how much time, money and people all of this will cost. Where will these resources come from? In this final step you will look at the roles of the candidate, campaign manager and other professionals you may have involved in your campaign. You will look at ways to recruit and keep volunteers. You will develop a campaign calendar and discuss scheduling. Finally, you will develop a campaign budget and figure out how the money will be raised.

8.2. The Role of the Candidate

The most important person in any political campaign is the candidate and the candidate's time is the most precious resource that the campaign has. If the candidate or the campaign wastes that time, it can never be replaced. It is therefore important to understand the role of the candidate and the best use of their time.

That role is very simple: meeting and persuading people. The most effective campaigner and fundraiser is the candidate. Voters and likely donors who personally meet the candidate and hear the message are much more likely to vote for that candidate and contribute to the campaign.

All too often, candidates enjoy sitting around their campaign headquarters plotting strategy with their teams or meeting with favorite supporters. Such candidates are wasting their time and are doomed to failure.

At the beginning of this treatise, it was suggested that your campaign hold a formal strategic planning session. Clearly, the candidate needs to be a part of this session and will have a great deal of impact on the basic strategy that is developed. Once the strategy has been decided, the candidate needs to leave the running of the campaign to the campaign director/manager and others and concentrate entirely on meeting and persuading as many voters as possible.

8.3.   The Role of the Campaign Director or Manager

The role of the campaign manager is to run the campaign. This must be someone in which the candidate has complete confidence. After all, this should be the most important thing in both of their lives for the relatively short period of time that the campaign will last. In a sense, the candidate is the heart of the campaign and the campaign director or manager is the brain. A good campaign needs both to be effective and efficient but they have very distinct roles to play.

Too often candidates want to run their own campaign. They either do not choose a campaign manager or choose someone they think they can manipulate. In either case they end up spending too much time making decisions that should be left to someone else, which takes time from their main job, meeting voters, volunteers and donors.

A campaign manager must make sure the candidate is scheduled to meet voters, they must deal with or otherwise supervise those who will deal with the press, the money, the other methods of voter contact and everything else planned (and unplanned) during the campaign.

8.4.   Campaign Professionals

Political campaigns, like anything else, benefit from experience. The more times an individual has been involved in past political campaigns, the better prepared they should be for the next political campaign. Having the advice, assistance or benefit of someone who has experienced the various phases of a campaign outlined in this handbook can be very helpful to a candidate and a campaign. It is one thing to understand the concept conveyed here and quite another to have experienced them in the heat of an intense campaign.

For that reason, political parties could greatly assist their candidates if they would maintain a list of experienced campaign directors or managers and others who have shown promise working on campaigns. The parties should develop these individuals and give them opportunities to work in campaigns so they are prepared for future campaigns.

Often there are people who have specialized in particular aspects of political campaigns. Political polling is one area that benefits from a great deal of experience and, if at all possible, a campaign should consider hiring someone who has this experience before they attempt to conduct a poll on their own. Politics has become very specialized and there are professionals who specialize in developing political direct mail or short message service (sms), political television and radio advertisements, compiling voters' lists, etc. All of these professionals can save the campaign a great deal of time (though they will cost money).

Yes, there are too many people who are passing themselves off as "image makers" and the like. Often with very little campaign experience, these individuals waste the candidate's time talking about psychoanalyzing the voters or changing the candidate's way of dressing. These people do not want to do the hard work of communicating a persuasive message to voters and lazy candidates who are looking for a quick fix often fall for their talk. They waste a lot of their time and money in doing so. Be careful of who you hire!

8.5. Campaign Structure

By this time you should have the beginning of a campaign plan drafted. Now you need to think about the structure and staff needed to implement the plan. You have the candidate and the campaign director/manager. Who else do you need to complete the campaign staffing? To determine this you should begin by looking at the voter contact plan. There are two concepts you may want to consider.

The first concept is that the structure is determined by tasks in the plan and accountability for those tasks. The only positions that need to be assigned are Campaign Director or Manager for oversight of all the operations, and someone to answer the phones and deal with general office functions. Other than that, there are no rules.

Suppose, for example, that your voter contact plan calls for signature collection, 4 press conferences, 5 literature drops to 60,000 households and 100 ward or district tours. In order to accomplish this, you will need to assign:

> 1 Campaign Manager
> 1 Office Manager or Administration Director (who answers phones, handles requests)
> 1 person responsible for drafting the literature and getting it printed (maybe half time position/maybe combined with press secretary position.)
> 2 people responsible for hiring temporary staff (same staff who handled signature collection and maybe election monitoring.)
> 60 temporary staff to distribute the literature of 500 pieces each in 2 days
> 100 ward or district coordinators responsible for coordination of voters and a scheduler officer.

On the other hand, if your plan's major effort will be persuading pensioners to vote for the candidate, then perhaps the structure would involve only:

❖ 1 Campaign manager responsible for oversight of the organizers
❖ 1 Office Manager
❖ 10 pensioner organizers in different locations responsible for signature collection, leafleting and meetings.

You will notice that in this last structure that there is no press secretary, fundraiser, scheduler nor assistants for each job. The jobs are closely following the plan. There is no room in your budget for excess people. You need a lean operation that will get the task done.

The second concept is that each job is defined by tasks assigned, not its title.

You should not think about titles, but hire and define jobs by the tasks that need to be completed. Then the staff members know their responsibilities and are held accountable for the tasks they are assigned. It also allows you to realistically assign tasks so that one person is not doing too much and another person is doing too little. There are too many campaigns where someone is an "assistant" or "deputy" in the office, and they are unable to give you a clear answer on what tasks they must accomplish on a daily basis.

In designing your structure, do not forget people who will volunteer to work on your campaign. Many family members and friends will volunteer full time in a staff position out of loyalty to the candidate. Additionally, many people will volunteer their time if the task were interesting or fun. Traveling with the candidate, doing research on the opposition, or helping with a rally are all tasks that are easy to get unpaid help. Tougher jobs like signature collection, door-to-door, image promotion and leafleting may need to be done by paid workers. Make sure you assign someone to be responsible for each task.

8.6.   Volunteers (People)

In developing your voter contact plan, you have probably realized that you cannot accomplish everything with the few people who started out helping on the campaign. If you are going to accomplish everything necessary you will need a lot of help and you probably will not be able to pay them. This is where volunteer support comes in. As your campaign begins persuading voters that you are the best candidate, it will also attract people who will offer even more support than their vote. These people will want to volunteer in the campaign and make sure you win.

People volunteer for many reasons. The first volunteers are often party loyalists who become involved out of a sense of commitment to the party. Some people volunteer because they feel strongly about a particular issue and either believes you agree with them on that issue or your opponent is really bad on that issue. Some people are just social and become involved with the political campaign because of friends or others who share their interests. Some people volunteer because they see this as an opportunity to get a job or some other gain. Finally some people volunteer because they seek recognition.

Volunteers stay with a campaign because they feel that they are making a contribution, feel appreciated, the work is interesting, they are meeting interesting people or it is fun. Volunteers can burn out if they are giving too much work but more likely they will leave the campaign because they became bored or feel that the work they are given does not matter.

Your first task is to determine how many volunteers you will need at which times to complete the objectives you have set for yourself. Again, you need to do the math.

For example, suppose you decide you want to deliver 3,000 pieces of literature in a particular neighborhood on a particular Saturday morning. You decide that one volunteer can deliver an average of 100 pieces of literature in an hour. Therefore it will take 30 volunteer hours to accomplish the job. You want to do the whole literature drop in three hours so you will need ten volunteers for three hours. You will also need to have the literature ready by Saturday, you will need to have some maps (visual representation) of the area and clear instructions for the volunteers and you will need to have someone responsible for overseeing the literature drop and knows what is supposed to happen. You may also have to provide transportation to the target neighborhood. Volunteers are just that, volunteers. You should recruit more than 10; say 15 or 20 in order to be certain of having 10 reliable volunteers at the appointed time.

You need to do this type of calculation for every part of your voter contact plan and the more detail you can provide the better. This is why planning is critical. In low budget, labor intensive campaigns there is often one person, a volunteer coordinator, who is responsible for recruiting and training volunteers, making sure they have the materials they need and making sure everything goes as planned.

Volunteers can come from many different areas. The first volunteers will probably be friends of the candidate and party activists who have worked on past campaigns. These will probably not be enough to accomplish everything and you will have to find many more people as the campaign builds in intensity. You should look for people who have volunteered in other areas of their life. They may volunteer for civic organizations, neighborhood groups, their religious organizations, unions, schools, etc. If your campaign message speaks to a particular issue or group you may be able to persuade an organization involved in that issue to support you and provide volunteers. As your campaign talks to voters you should take every opportunity to ask people to help the campaign. Always have volunteer cards such as the one found in Appendix F available and ready for people who express strong support.

8.7. Worksheet 11: Budgeting Volunteers

❖ List all the voter contact activities your campaign intends to accomplish. Be as specific as possible, using real numbers. How many pieces of literature do you need to deliver? How many phone calls do you need to make and how many phones do you have available? How many homes do you want to visit in how much time?

❖ Next, determine how many volunteers you will need to reasonably accomplish each task you have listed above. How much of the task can one volunteer accomplish in one hour and how many volunteer hours will it take to accomplish the whole job?

❖ Finally, estimate how many volunteers you will need throughout the campaign. Often you will be able to use the same volunteers for different tasks at different times. In other cases a volunteer who is good at making phone calls may not be as good at putting up signs. Remember that you will need to recruit twice as many volunteers as your estimate need for a particular task.

8.8. Scheduling and Calendar (Time)

From the very beginning of the campaign you have probably been collecting various dates that will be important to your campaign. Election Day is one obvious important date. Other important dates may be filing deadlines, campaign start date and dates when you are required by law to make certain reports.

All of these dates should be kept on a master campaign calendar. Early in the campaign this may be a monthly calendar but as Election Day draws closer, you may want to develop a weekly or even daily calendar that provides more details.

We will add to this calendar any important events or meetings that the candidate must attend. Your campaign will have to develop a system for dealing with invitations. This system should include ways to decide if an event is important enough to attend and ways to decline invitations that the campaign decides are not important.

Next you will add all of the various voter contact activities. Here it is important to distinguish between activities that will require the candidate and those that will be handled by the campaign and volunteers. Because certain voter contact activities will happen over a long period of time and overlap with other activities. It is also necessary to develop a timeline of events that will provide more details about time, money and people involved in each activity.

In larger campaigns, the responsibility for all of this would be assigned to a scheduler. In smaller campaigns this maybe one of the responsibilities that the campaign manager will handle. Again, it is important that the candidate not keep their own calendar because this often leads to confusion about who needs to be where and when.

8.9.   Worksheet 12: Calendar

Develop a master calendar for the campaign that will include all the important dates and all the important activities of the campaign. Assign one person to be responsible for keeping the calendar up to date and distributing it to everyone in the campaign who needs to keep abreast of the activities. Develop a system for dealing with invitations, deciding whether or not the candidate will attend, and whether a letter of acceptance or regrets has been sent. You will also want to collect all the important information about the event, such as the contact person with their phone number, what the candidate will do at the event, directions to the event, etc.

Time	Sunday	Monday	Tuesday	Wednesday	Thursday	Friday	Saturday

8.10.   Worksheet 13: Timeline

The following sample timeline is an excellent tool for helping your campaign plan its voter contact activities. This sample timeline shows the last weeks of the campaign. Fill out a similar timeline for your campaign from beginning to the end. In doing so, you should consider the following rules:

❖ You should start your voter contact planning from Election Day and work backwards. On the day the campaign period ends, what will you have needed to accomplish in order to win? How many posters will you have to put up? How many brochures will you have to have distributed? How many doors should you and your supporters have knocked on?

❖ All of your voter contact activities should be quantifiable. Your voter contact goals should not include "establishing good media relations" because such a goal does not mean anything in real terms. How many events will you hold? How many press releases will you send out? You should quantify everything for two reasons:

- Quantifiable goals will help you measure the progress of your campaign. If by December 10th your team has knocked on 5,000 doors, is that good or bad? If your goal is 6,000, it's good; if your goal is 60,000, it's bad. If you have not set a quantifiable goal, you have no idea.

- Quantifiable goals will help your budgeting process. You cannot reasonable compare the relative costs and benefits of brochures vs. posters vs. radio adverts unless you know how many of each you are talking about.

❖ For each goal, plan the activities that will be required to reach that goal. If you plan to put up 5,000 posters by December 1st, by what date should you take your poster design to the printer? When should you recruit the people necessary to put up 5,000 posters?

❖ Do not forget to plan for the resources you will need to accomplish each activity. As you look at your timeline, figure out for each week how many people and how much money you will need for the activities planned for that week. Where will the resources come from?

❖ Plan your timeline within the framework of the election law. Does your specific election law specify certain dates by which certain activities must be accomplished and dates before which other activities are prohibited?

Date	Activity	Responsible Person	Expenses
After Election Day	Summing up results and Payment of workers	Campaign Director/ Manager, Campaign Team & Finance Director	
Election Day (ED)	Observers at 1765 Polling Stations	Volunteer Coordinator	
ED	Candidate Scheduled Visits with Press	Scheduler	
Election Day minus 1 Day (ED - 1)	Volunteers distribute 1500 pieces of last minute literature in 3 swing constituency or districts	Volunteer Coordinator, 3 Constituency/District Coordinators and 300 Volunteers	
ED –2	Observer Training Distribute last minute literature to volunteers	Volunteer Coordinator	
ED – 2	Last Mailing in the mail boxes	Campaign Manager	
ED - 6 through ED - 1	Phoning of known supporters reminding them to go vote	Volunteer Coordinator and 100 Volunteers	
ED - 6	Printing of 3000 pieces of last minute literature	Campaign Manager	
ED - 5	Second to last Mailing in the mail boxes	Campaign Manager	
ED - 7 through ED - 1	Candidate goes door to door in last Constituency/ District - 300 contacts	Candidate, Three Assistants and Scheduler	
ED - 7	Last Mailing sent	Campaign Manager	
ED - 10	Second to last Mailing sent	Campaign Manager	
ED - 14	Last Mailing of 1000 pieces goes to Printer	Campaign Manager	
ED - 14 through ED - 7	Candidate goes door to door in second to last constituency/district - 300 contacts	Candidate, Three Assistants and Scheduler	
ED - 17	Second to last Mailing of 1000 pieces goes to Printer	Campaign Manager	

Source: National Democratic Institute for International Affairs (2009).

8.11. Computers

Using computers can save the campaign on all three resources - time, money and people. Many of the most basic things you do in politics - analyze data, keep track of and contact people, and communicate a message - can either be done efficiently with a personal computer or aided with the use of a personal computer. You can use spreadsheet programs to analyze data from past elections. You can use database programs to maintain lists of voters and record who supports your candidate. You can maintain and quickly update a campaign calendar using calendar programs. For writing, use word processing and desktop publishing programs. Short message service (sms), e-mail and web sites can aid in communicating the message to the media and opinion leaders.

Once the campaign has decided what it hopes to accomplish and how it will achieve its objectives, it will be better able to determine how computers can make things easier.

8.12. The Coordinated Campaign with Your Party

Many of the tasks an individual campaign needs to accomplish can be done much more efficiently or less expensively if they can be coordinated with other similar campaigns. Coordinating these efforts and achieving these savings should be the role of a political party in an election cycle. Your campaign may be expected to help the party achieve its objectives as well. Your campaign should clearly understand what the party expects from you and what you can expect from the party.

Often candidates think that the central party organization should for some reason fund their campaign and their voter contact relies on the visit of the party leader to their region. In most cases there is not enough money at the national level to fund everyone's campaign and the national leader cannot go everywhere. Besides, a campaign that cannot raise its own funds and relies on the party leader to contact its voters is probably not organized enough or worth the effort.

The following are some of the areas where the party may help:

8.12.1. Message and information

Your political party should have an overall message of why voters should support its candidates. Assuming you agree with this message and your individual message corresponds to this national message, the party may be able to provide you with general material. Your national party may provide information about policy initiatives at the national level or negative information about your opponents. Sometimes parties have elected officials "adopt" first time candidates to help with problems, questions, and anxious moments.

8.12.2. Material design

Often national parties will be able to help you design your campaign materials so that they match the national message. The party may contract with printers and other vendors to produce all or much of the materials, thus gaining a saving in price for all its candidates. You also may be able to re-use national party materials, simply adding your name or local information. This is only where national party lends hands of credence.

8.12.3. National materials

The national party can provide posters, leaflets and platforms, and you may ask if it is possible for them to keep a blank space so your campaign can print or put stickers of your candidate's name. Sometimes national leaflets are printed on one side and your campaign can print on the back (to save money for your campaign.) In addition, you may ask for buttons, posters, and calendars that you can sell or give to people who are contributors or volunteers. (Be careful not to violate Election Law provisions.) This is only where national party lends hands of credence.

8.12.4. Press

The national office should also let you know about national press events that your campaign can use to get local attention. The party's response to a national crisis would be valuable to have in a timely manner, to get press attention at the local level.

8.12.5. Visits

The visit of the national party leader can often draw local attention to your campaign; nevertheless this should not be your only strategy. Too often local parties and local candidates expect the national party and the national leader to come do their work for them. This is just a sign of laziness and probably means that it isn't worth the effort from the capital.

If the national leader does come, you will have a lot of work to do preparing for the visit. You will have to make sure you have a good turnout of supporters and press so that the trip is not a wasted effort or worse, an embarrassment. Make sure that the visit does not cost the campaign too much in time, money and people. All of the benefits of a visit can be squandered if it pulls the campaign off schedule or uses too many non-budgeted resources.

If the national leader cannot come, you may want to request a surrogate or other major figure to come and endorse your candidacy. Many candidates will be busy with their own campaigns, but others will not have much of a race and can make a short day trip. For all events with national party leaders, local candidates should be on the dais or stage and introduced during the event. These are also good opportunities to collect names and phone numbers of potential supporters.

8.12.6. Endorsements

At your next event, get photos of your candidate with national party leaders that can be used in campaign materials. Just as important is getting a commitment of party leaders to help your efforts. For example, if one of your targeted groups is working women, ask if a well-known female legislator can draft a letter to your constituents about the importance of electing your candidate.

8.13. Building a Coalition and Outreach to Civic Organizations

Civic organizations can play an important role in your election campaign. While the development of civic organizations may be relatively low, there has been active, positive political participation by civic organizations in various election campaigns.

You should make a list of the civic groups in your constituency or district that could be supportive; think not only of officially registered groups, but also "informal organizations" such as church groups, work places, and universities that you can reach through opinion leaders. Using your demographic targeting may give you ideas for possible supportive groups.

Cultivation of civic organizations should be done in the early stages of the campaign, when the candidate has time to meet with their leadership to ask for support. You must allow time for your relationships to grow for the civic support to be effective.

Civic groups may help your campaign in a number of ways.

8.13.1. Endorsement

Simply by announcing that an organization supports your candidate can often be a boost to your campaign. You may be able to use the organization's name on your posters or literature. This support is particularly effective if the organization is well known and respected.

8.13.2. Mobilize membership

Once the endorsement is made, ask the group to contact their membership either by phone or through a mailing or newsletter to announce their support and recruit supporters for concrete campaign tasks such as signature collection, door to door canvassing, etc.

8.13.3. Press events

There are a number of press activities civic organizations can provide your campaign. For example, they can organize a press conference announcing their support of you, and at this time they can speak out against your opponents. It is often more credible if a group or someone other than the campaign delivers a negative message about the opponent. Civic organizations can send out press releases repeating their support, as issues of specific concern to them arise during the campaign.

8.13.4. Research

A civic organization can provide information in their area of expertise and help research the impact of legislation on the community. In addition, they can draft position papers, provide "talking points" to a candidate, or even help prepare speeches on issues they are concerned about. Civic organizations can also help with opposition research by identifying when your opponents have made statements or voted against their interests.

8.13.5. Public events

When a civic group is holding an event, ask them to circulate a sign-up sheet for people interested in supporting your campaign; a group can even hold an event on your behalf. If your campaign is holding a rally, fundraiser, or press conference, ask the group to turn out their membership for the event.

8.13.6. Outreach

Civic group leaders can often help introduce you to other groups and opinion leaders. Use their contacts to persuade other groups to support or endorse your campaign.

Rules for working with civic organizations

In your work with civic organizations, bear in mind the following rules:

➢ Ask for concrete, quantifiable contributions to your campaign. One thousand petition signatures will help you a lot more that the vague promise of support.

➢ Verify that the civic group is really doing what it said it would do. You do not want to fail to register your candidacy because you relied on the promise of 100,000 signatures that result in only 50,000 signatures.

➢ Remember that your relationship with civic groups is a two-way street. If you do not go out of your way to help your supporters, they may not be there the next time you need their help. A good rule to follow with civic organizations is "under promise and over deliver."

8.14. Worksheet 14: Working With Civic Organizations and Your Party

❖ Make a list of all the civic groups and other organizations that should be supportive of your campaign. List the contact person with each organization, the phone number and any other information that would be helpful in making contact with the group.

❖ Reviewing your list of voter contact and other campaign activities, decide how these organizations and your party could best be of assistance to your campaign. Keeping in mind that coalition building is a two-way street, what will each of your partners expect from you in return for their assistance?

8.15. Campaign Budgeting (Money 1)

Just about everything you do in the campaign will cost something. You should estimate how much each of the tasks you hope to accomplish will cost and develop an overall budget for the entire campaign. Your campaign budget should not be a wish list, but a realistic list of what will be needed to implement your campaign plan. Written budgets are the only tools for tracking expenditures, providing goals for fundraisers, and keeping the candidate and campaign from spending without thinking.

Review your timeline and calendar to determine at what point in the campaign you will need the money. By organizing your budget month-by-month or even week-by-week, you will be able to anticipate what amounts you will need at what time. You will thus avoid the age-old problem of cash flow difficulties, and your fundraisers will understand what money is needed at what time.

Having high, medium, and low budget plans is useful in case your fundraising does not go as well as anticipated. You can better plan and save money for spending priorities like voter contact activities.

Campaigns everywhere need to spend the bulk of their funds on voter contact activities. Administrative costs, including office machines, office staff, and phones, should be less than 20% of your budget. Voter contact costs, including television, printed materials, and door-to-door workers should consume 70% to 80% of your financial resources. Research, including polling, should take up less than 10% of your budget.

8.16. Worksheet 15: Developing a Budget

❖ Review all of your voter contact and other campaign activities and determine an estimated cost for each item to determine an overall budget.

❖ Review the calendar and determine when you will need to make payments to develop a cash flow budget. Add all of these dates to the master calendar.

8.17. Campaign Fundraising (Money 2)

Fundraising is the process of systematically collecting names of potential contributors and then identifying why that potential contributor would give money, how much they can give, and who is the best person from the campaign to ask for the money. Every campaign budget needs a companion fundraising plan to understand what amount of money needs to be raised and when.

The candidate and the campaign should target donors in the same way that they target voters. There are two important factors to remember about people who may contribute to your campaign. First, unlike voters who can only vote once for your candidate in this election (and therefore are equal to all other voters), the contributors can give varying amounts. The second point is that while voters have to live within the constituency or district, contributors can live almost anywhere. So while you will probably receive a lot fewer donations than you do vote, you are able to look for these contributors just about anywhere.

Just as with recruiting volunteers, there are different reasons why people will contribute. For each type of contributor you will need to expend varying degrees of time and effort required gaining their support.

The first group is family, personal friends and close professional colleagues. These people will give because they know the candidate personally.

The second group is people who will directly benefit from the election of the candidate. These may be people who have a financial relationship with the candidate, a financial stake in the election of the candidate or those who believe their own personal power will increase through the election of the candidate.

The third group is people who share the candidate's ideological view. Often these are members of the same organizations that the candidate is a member of or organizations that the candidate associates with.

The final group is people who disagree with your opponent or want to see your opponent defeated. These people may not agree with your candidate but see your campaign as a vehicle to make a point about how bad your opponent has been on a particular issue or for some other reasons want to stop your opponent from winning.

The most important reason why people do not give to political campaigns is that they were never asked to give. Too often candidates feel they "know" that someone will not give or cannot afford to give and therefore do not ask them. This is often just an excuse to avoid asking and thereby avoid raising money.

For each potential contributor, you should determine how best to ask for money. Will that person give at a meeting with the candidate or a friend of the campaign? Would they like to attend an event? Should they be sent some general information and followed up with a phone call or meeting with the candidate?

In many cases the best person to ask for money is the candidate. Candidates need to know that they are not "begging" for money. Rather they are asking their supporters to "invest" in the campaign, a campaign in which they are often investing a lot of their own time and money. If it is worth it to the candidate to get elected, why shouldn't it be worth it to the supporters?

Of course, the most difficult part of fundraising is asking. The person asking should practice beforehand with a member of the campaign who then brings up every excuse not to give. By "practicing" this way, the fundraiser is more prepared.

In your fundraising activities, you should bear in mind the following rules:

❖ If the contributor does not support an issue or your party, try to keep the conversation on the issues and concerns, you both have in common.

❖ Ask for a specific amount. It is better to ask for a slightly higher amount and flatter them, than to ask for a very low amount and get smaller contributions.

❖ Ask how and when the money will be available to have someone pick up. This "collection" is the most important piece, because you do not want people ducking away from commitments two months later. The faster you can get the money into your hands the better.

❖ Never ever forget to say thank you. This is best (and the cheapest) way to make sure the contributor knows that their contribution is appreciated, no matter how small. Possibly, send an acknowledgement letters to them.

Events or parties are used by many campaigns that often involve a national leader or a celebrity. People are more likely to give if the event sounds fun, interesting and has an attraction. You will avoid big fights if you work out with the national office whether the funds raised at the event will go to the national effort, will be split with your campaign, or will go entirely to the campaign.

Fundraising letters are a great way to get information on the candidate to potential contributors. You may not want to ask for money in the letter, because it is very easy to say no and throw out a letter. It is much harder to say no and throw out a person, so write in your letter that someone from the campaign will be following up with a phone call or meeting request. This way your campaign can ask for a specific amount, and respond to any concern the contributor has. The campaign should follow up on the letter just days after the letter arrives, so do not mail out more letters than someone can follow-up with.

The exception to this is if you are sending out fundraising letters to very small contributors, where you will not be embarrassed if the press writes a story about how you are relying on contributions from citizen donations. Also leaflets and mailing should always say at the bottom, "Our campaign relies on small contributions and volunteering from citizens like you. If you will like to help call our line or stop by our office (remember to state the phone line and street numbers)." There will not be hundreds of responses, but you may get a number of contributions.

Never pass up an opportunity to raise money. Remember that fundraising is not mandatory for your campaign, though families, friends and colleagues are likely to give financial supports.

8.18.   Worksheet 15: Developing a Fundraising Plan

❖ Start by having the candidate list every member of their family, all of their close friends and any close professional colleagues. They should also want to list anyone who would directly benefit from their election. The candidate should then write the amount of a contribution they could expect to receive next to each name. Every person on this first list must have some amount of money next to their name.

❖ Begin putting together lists of people who are active in organizations that represent your target audience. These may be neighborhood organizations, unions, business organizations, etc. You should also consider lists of organizations and people who may want to see your opponent defeated and would consider your campaign a vehicle to make this happen. For this list determine who can best ask these individuals to contribute to your campaign and how much each person can be expected to give.

❖ For all of these lists, determine what must be done to access money from these potential donors. You may have to acquire lists with phone numbers, find members of the particular group who already support your campaign, etc.

❖ Determine how best to solicit contributions from the targeted donors. This maybe a personal call from the candidate, a call from a member of the organization, a phone call or letter from the campaign, or attendance at an event.

8.19.   The Constant Campaign

There are a lot of tasks that must be completed over the course of the campaign. A few of these tasks must wait until the campaign is underway. Many of these tasks, such as all forms of voter persuasion, will be more effective if they are done closer to Election Day. However, voter persuasion and many other tasks can be made much easier if they are started well in advance of the actual campaign. Some of the tasks, such as analyzing past elections, can be completed years before the campaign begins.

Elected officials, potential candidates and political parties would benefit greatly if they would start viewing the political campaign as an ongoing, constant process. The next campaign begins the day after the last election. Leaving all of the work of campaigning until the election cycle begins makes all the work much more difficult and decreases the chances that any of this work will be done well.

Below is a partial list of tasks that your campaign may have to complete and suggestions about whether or not you can begin the task before the actual campaign begins. You may want to add to this list or adapt it to your particular situation.

Campaign Task	When To Start
Research election laws	The party and potential candidates should know the current law early in the campaign and keep abreast of any changes.
Constituency/ District targeting	Political parties should select constituencies/districts where they want to concentrate their efforts well in advance of the campaign and evaluate this targeting as the election progresses.
Constituency/ District research	Political parties and potential candidates should begin gathering information on election constituencies/districts well in advance of the campaign.
Voter research	Political parties and potential candidates should begin gathering information on voter preferences as soon as possible and monitor changes throughout the campaign.
Research past elections	As soon as the last election is over or well in advance of the campaign.
Research this election	The campaign should access the current political situation as soon as it is known and monitor it throughout the campaign.
Candidate selection	Political parties should begin recruiting and researching potential candidates well in advance of the campaign.
Registering the candidate	There is often a limited window within the law of when the candidacy can be officially registered.
Putting together a campaign committee	Once the candidate has decided to run, they should begin putting together a group of individuals that will help make the campaign happen.
Research candidates	The campaign should conduct detailed research on all aspects of their candidate as soon as the candidate decides to run.

Research opposition candidates	As soon as the opposition is known.
Setting a goal	The campaign should determine how many votes it will need to win as soon as possible and monitor for any changes to this number throughout the campaign.
Targeting the voters	The political party or campaign organization should determine whom their base voters are well before the campaign begins. The campaign should decide which voters is their target audience as soon as possible and monitor this throughout the campaign.
Developing a campaign message	Political parties should have a basic message that they are constantly delivering and monitoring the impact. The candidate and campaign should develop a message as soon as possible.
Developing a voter contact plan	Once the campaign has completed the research and developed the message, it needs to decide how it will deliver this message.
Developing a campaign timeline	The campaign should begin developing a basic timeline as soon as possible and add to it as the campaign progresses.
Writing a campaign plan	The campaign plan should be written as soon as possible.
Developing a campaign budget	Once the campaign knows what it intends to accomplish, it should develop a budget of what will be needed in terms of time, money and people to achieve these goals.
Fundraising	Once the candidate decides to run they should begin raising the money needed. This will most likely continue throughout the campaign.
Monitoring the cash flow	The campaign will have to constantly monitor how the money is being spent.
Hiring campaign staff	The candidate should hire staff as soon as they are needed.
Opening a headquarters	The campaign should open a headquarters when it is needed.

Developing a press strategy	The press strategy should be part of the overall voter contact plan and should be developed more specifically as soon as possible.
Speech writing	Speech writing should be done as needed.
Building a coalition	The political parties should begin developing a coalition with civic organizations well in advance of the election. The campaign should make contact and begin working with civic organizations as soon as possible.
Getting endorsements	The schedule for endorsements is often in the control of the organization that may provide the endorsement. Still, the campaign needs to know this schedule and do what is necessary to earn the desired endorsements.
Scheduling the candidate	Scheduling is done as needed. The campaign should develop a system for responding to invitations and maintaining a schedule as soon as possible.
Staffing the candidate	Staffing will be done as needed. In most cases, the candidate should have someone with them at all times.
Dealing with vendors	Once the campaign plan is written, the campaign will need to start dealing with vendors to accomplish the objectives.
Recruiting volunteers	Recruiting volunteers should begin early and happen throughout the campaign. Political parties or campaign organization should maintain a database of past volunteers and activists.
Developing campaign materials	Once the message is developed and the method of voter contact is decided upon, the campaign should start developing materials.
Implementing the voter contact plan	Once the voter contact method is decided upon, the campaign must put all of its effort into implementing the plan. There should also be contact with voters well in advance of the campaign.
Responding to voter requests	Responding to voter requests should be on going for both the party and the campaign.

Source: National Democratic Institute for International Affairs (2009).

National Democratic Institute for International Affairs (2009). Political Campaign Planning Manual, A step by step guide to winning elections, Washington, DC: NDI.

CHAPTER NINE

CONCLUSION

The success or failure of candidates to win election or political parties to form government after election will depend on the campaign strategy. If you are a candidate contesting for the first time, seeking re-election or re-contesting, you will not be successful if you fail to have in place a winning strategy for a successful political election campaign. Even political parties who wish to muster the numbers to form government must bear in mind that if you fail to prepare, you are preparing to fail. If you fail to prepare, your time and resources will be wasted and you will not realize your aspiration.

This handbook provides a great deal of information. Even if you read through the handbook first and then work through it step by step, taking the time to write a campaign plan, there are probably still important points you will miss. It is impossible to foresee all that will happen in the campaign, even if you have past political experience. You should refer back to this handbook, just as you should refer back to your campaign plan, as the campaign progresses and questions arise.

The most important concepts are the following:

- ✓ You must begin to look at the campaign as a whole and then break it down into easy to accomplish parts.
- ✓ You must develop a realistic strategy for winning and you must write that strategy down in a realistic campaign plan.

✓ Finally, you must follow through on that campaign plan, doing the hard work of contacting voters and persuading them.

Following these steps will make your campaign much more efficient at using your resources of time, money and people. Following these steps will make your campaign much more effective at persuading voters to vote for you. Following these steps will start you well on the road to victory and election glory.

National Democratic Institute for International Affairs (2009). Political Campaign Planning Manual, A step by step guide to winning elections, Washington, DC: NDI.

APPENDIX A

A GLOSSARY OF CAMPAIGN TERMS

Advertisements - A form of voter contact in which the campaign pays to have the mass media deliver the message. See Message, Mass Media and Paid Media.

Attitudes - This describes how the voters feel going into the election - either satisfied or angry, feeling better off or worse off, etc.

Ballot - The official document voters will use to cast their vote, thus making their choices known.

Ballot Placement - This is the place where the candidate's name appears on the ballot. If there are a lot of candidates on the ballot or it is otherwise long, voters will often not read all the way down the list, thus giving candidates with a higher placement a better chance.

Baseline Poll - A political poll taken to determine as much information about the voters as possible, usually done early in the campaign before there is much political activity. See Political Poll and Tracking Poll.

Blind Pull - In areas where there is considerable support for the candidate - say seven out of ten voters support the candidate - it may benefit the campaign if as many voters as possible go to the polls, regardless of whether or not the supporters have been identified. If everyone in an area is encouraged to vote, then this is considered a "blind pull" to the polls. See GOTV and Pull.

Bottleneck - The term used to describe the individual, place or position that causes the flow of information or other activities to slow down or halt.

Budget - The budget usually refers to the amount of money you expect to spend on various aspects of the campaign. You should also figure out how many people are needed to accomplish each task and how long each task will take. In this way you will also be budgeting time and people resources as well.

By-Election - An election not held at the usually scheduled time, often to fill a vacancy in the office. There is often much lower voter turnout in a special or by-election. See Special Election.

Campaign Calendar - The calendar used to schedule events and voter contact in the campaign. This should be a master calendar with the final say of what goes on in the campaign ("if it is not on the calendar, it is not happening"). Often there is a large, public version (and therefore less complete) hanging on the wall.

Campaign Committee - Often this is the decision making group in the campaign made up of the key advisors to the candidate. See Campaign Team.

Campaign Director (Manager) - The person responsible for overseeing the strategic development and the day-to-day running of the campaign. The candidate cannot be the campaign director/manager.

Campaign Goal - Any political action to put a candidate in office or to win election.

Campaign Literature - Printed campaign material used to inform potential voters about the candidate and persuade them to vote for the candidate.

Campaign Methods - There are no tricks or fancy techniques to winning the confidence of the voters. There is only hard work and the methods outlined in this handbook.

Campaign Plan - The written document bringing together the important research, the message, the targeting and the strategy of the campaign. This should be drafted at the beginning of the campaign and provide a step-by-step outline of how the campaign will get to Election Day.

Campaign Professionals - People who have experience working in many past campaigns and are often paid to work on campaigns. These people understand the hard work needed to persuade voters and get elected. There are no tricks or short cuts.

Campaign Resources - The only resources available in politics are time, money and people. Everything can be divided into one of these areas. It is important that every campaign, no matter how large or small, use each of these resources in the most efficient manner possible.

Campaign Team - Often this is the decision making group in the campaign made up of the key advisors to the candidate. In some cases the Campaign Team maybe the Campaign Committee plus the campaign staff. See Campaign Committee.

Candidate - This is the person running for a particular elected position. The role of the candidate is to meet voters and potential donors to the campaign and persuade them to support the candidate. The candidate cannot be the campaign director or manager, responsible for the strategic development and day to day running of the campaign.

Candidate Research - Candidate research is all the information, both good and bad, that your campaign can put together on your candidate. This is part of the overall research that should be done at the beginning of the campaign. See Research.

Canvass - Going from door to door, house-to-house, apartment-to-apartment, voter-to-voter, delivering the campaign message persuading voters and identifying supporters. See Door-to-Door.

Characteristics of Message - A campaign message must be short, truthful and credible, persuasive and important to voters, show contrast with the opposition, and speak to the heart, be targeted and repeated again and again.

Coffee Program - A series of "coffees" or small events in various homes of supporters over the course of the campaign. These are labor and time intensive and often require a full time person who organizes them. See Coffees.

Coffees - These are events in the home of a volunteer or supporter where their friends are able to meet the candidate. These have the advantage of face-to-face contact with the candidate, the most persuasive form of voter contact. Coffees can also be used for small donor fundraising. See Coffee Program.

Collateral Group - A demographic group similar to or having similar interests to another demographic group. For example, teachers may share an interest in improving education with mothers. Teachers and mothers would be collateral groups.

Constant Campaign - The concept that the candidate and the party are always working for the next election and do not wait for election time to start delivering a message.

Constituency - A portion of the population represented by a particular elected leader or organization.

Contrast - Using the campaign message to demonstrate the difference between candidates when they are compared with each other. It is important to give the voters a clear choice. See Credibility and Message.

Contributions - Money donated to a political campaign or otherwise given without conditions.

Created Events - Any attempt to bring together a large group of people by the campaign. Generally people brought together by the campaign will already be supporters, but the event may receive press coverage and thereby influence other voters. Created events can also be used to raise funds and energize supporters. See Preset Events.

Credibility - The positive or negative view voters have of a candidate or party. By creating contrast, campaigns can use their message to raise their candidate's credibility, lower their opponents' credibility or both. See Contrast and Message.

Cross Tabs - Comparing or referencing various responses to questions on a political poll with responses to other questions or demographic information. The real information is a political poll comes from the cross tabs. See Political Poll.

Cross-sets - Small groupings within the demographic breakdown that are members of at least two other demographic sets.

Demographic Targeting - Grouping of the voting population based on age, gender, income, education level, occupation, ethnic background, religion, or any other smaller, identifiable grouping of the whole voter population. It is assumed that voters who identify with a particular demographic group will vote in a similar way.

Direct Voter Contact - Any method by which the candidate or the campaign communicates the message to potential voters in person, rather than using some form of media.

Direct Mail Fundraising - Sending voters something in the mail asking them to contribute to an organization, a political party or a candidate.

District - The defined geographic area in which the election will be held and following the election, the winner will represent. See Constituency.

District Research - District research is all the information that your campaign can put together about the district. This is part of the overall research that should be done at the beginning of the campaign. See Research.

Door-to-Door - This is a type of voter contact in which the candidate or volunteers go from one house or apartment to another, talking directly to voters. When done by the candidate, this is one of the most persuasive methods of winning votes, though it is time and labor intensive.

Earned Media - Any coverage of the campaign in the press. It is called "earned media," as opposed to paid media, because the campaign will often have to expend a considerable amount of time and energy to receive good coverage.

Election Commission - Usually a non-partisan board set up to oversee the election and make sure that it is conducted fairly. See Board of Elections.

Election Day - The day on which the voters come to the polls and cast their votes to elect their leaders.

Election Goal - This usually refers to the number of votes needed to win an election. It is assumed that the overall goal of the election campaign is to win a particular office. This is not always the case. Some candidates run for office to promote a particular idea or expose an opponent's record on a particular issue.

Election Rules - Any laws or rules of the election commission that will affect the election in any way.

Election Technologies - This term often refers to complicated ideas or "tricks" for convincing voters to vote for the candidate. There are no tricks and the campaign methods outlined here are not complicated. They only require a lot of hard work, day after day. See Campaign Methods.

Electorate - This is the portion of the population able to vote in this election. See Voters.

Electronic Media - Electronic media is television and radio organizations that use spoken words and/or video, as opposed to the print media that uses the written word and/or pictures. See Print Media and Mass Media.

Endorsements - Endorsements are announced or written support for the candidate from opinion leaders or organizations that will influence members of their organizations or other voters to vote for the candidate. See Opinion Leaders.

Ethnic Voter - An ethnic voter is one who identifies with a particular national, religious or language grouping. These are generally groupings within the demographic breakdown of the population.

Executive Office - An elected position that oversees the running of the government, such as a governor or president. See Legislative Office.

Expected Turnout - The number of voters you believe will go to the polls and vote in any particular election and race.

Field Director - A person on the campaign staff responsible for organizing the direct contact with the voters by the candidate and the volunteers.

Filing Deadline - The last day and time in which the candidate can file for a particular office.

Focus Groups - A method of sociological research in which a small group of people are brought together and asked a series of questions. The point is to receive qualitative information about public attitudes and test reactions to various messages and information. See Political Polling.

Friends of Friends Program - A method of voter contact where volunteers agree to contact their friends either through the mail or on the phone and encourage them to vote for the candidate.

Fundraiser - An event planned with the goal of raising money for the campaign. Fundraiser may also refer to the person who raises the funds for the campaign by any method.

Fundraising - Any method used to raise money for the campaign.

Geographic Targeting - Grouping the voting population based on where they live and determining patterns within the voting population based on geography. It is assumed that voters who live in a particular area and voted one way in the past will probably vote the same way in the future, barring any extreme change in their situation.

Golden Rule - All campaigns must repeatedly communicate a persuasive message to people who will vote.

GOTV - "Get Out The Vote" or GOTV is the term used to remind voters to go to the polls and vote for your candidate. Often a campaign will expend a considerable amount of effort just before Election Day to make sure that your supporters turn out and vote. See Pull and Blind Pull.

High Profile Race - An election campaign for a particular office that voters are interested in and want to hear about. High profile races often receive the most votes. See Low Profile Race.

Horserace Question - A question on a political poll that asks, "if the election were held today, would you vote for candidate A or candidate B." This type of information is often of little use to the campaign because it does not provide a reason for the decision. The only horserace question that counts is at the polls on Election Day. See Political Polling.

Image Maker - There are a lot of people with very little campaign experience who are conning candidates into thinking that elections are complicated or that there are certain tricks they can use to fool the voters. They often talk about psychoanalyzing the voters or the way a candidate dresses instead of the hard work of contacting voters and persuading them with a clear message. Lazy candidates who are looking for a quick fix often fall for their talk and waste a lot of time and money in doing so. See Campaign Professionals.

Incumbent - A candidate running again for an elected position that they already hold.

Internet Campaigning - Any method of voter contact using computers and the communications network. Typically this involves developing campaign pages on the World Wide Web. While this can be an inexpensive way to convey a lot of information to those interested in the candidate and the campaign, it is not an effective voter contact method because it does not go to the voters. Instead voters have to go to it.

Issues - A solution or partial solution to a problem. The economic crisis is a problem, not an issue. Whether or not cutting taxes to spur investment or paying pensions are good ideas may be issues.

Kitchen Cabinet - A term used to describe the key advisors to a candidate informally organized so as not to attract attention.

Lawn Signs - Large signs with the candidate's name on them and the office they are seeking which can be put on lawns and other areas near roads. Lawn signs are good for increasing name recognition of the candidate and reminding people to vote. See Visibility.

Leadership Qualities - The particular traits people are looking for in those that represent them.

Legislative Office - A legislative office is a position on an elected council, congress, assembly or other body dealing with legislation. See Executive Office.

Literature Drop - A voter contact method in which volunteers go door to door to leave campaign literature at each house or apartment of voters in the constituency or district. Because they do not knock on the doors and talk to voters, this is a less persuasive method of voter contact than door to door, but can be accomplished a lot quicker. See Campaign Literature and Door-to-Door.

Literature Handout - A voter contact method in which volunteers hand campaign literature to potential voters gathered in any large groups, such as workers leaving a factory, commuters waiting for a bus or train or shoppers at a market. See Campaign Literature.

Low Profile Race - An election campaign for a particular office that voters are not that interested in and they are likely to ignore. See High Profile Race and Down Ballot.

Mail - A voter contact method in which campaign literature is sent through the post or e-mail to voters. Depending on the type of voter file or mailing list you have, this literature can be targeted to voters based on geography or demographics. See Campaign Literature and Voter File.

Majority - Fifty percent of the votes cast plus one vote. This as opposed to a simple plurality of the vote or the most votes cast. See Plurality.

Margin of Victory - The number of votes needed to assure that the candidate wins the election. See Targeting.

Mass Media - Any independent press that has a large audience.

Media Market - The geographic area reached by the mass media in a particular region. Often a newspaper will have a circulation within a city and its metropolitan area and a television station can only reach a certain area.

Message - A limited body of truthful information that is consistently conveyed by the candidate and the campaign to provide persuasive reasons for voters to vote for the candidate.

Message Box - The exercise in which the campaign views what will be said in the election by us about us, by us about them, by them about them and by them about us. This should be a fairly complete picture of everything that will be said during the campaign and should provide the campaign with a clear contrast with their opponents.

Money - One of the three resources in every political campaign, the others being time and people. It is important to determine how much money each activity in the campaign will cost and plan for it. See Campaign Resources and Budget.

Multi Mandate - An election district in which more than one candidate will win the positions sought in the campaign.

Murphy's Law - "Anything that can go wrong will go wrong."

Name Recognition - Identification of the candidate's name by the voters. Often voters will know little about the candidates and therefore vote for the name that they recognize. It is important for candidates to have the voters associate their name with their message and party because only the name or party logo will appear on the ballot.

Non-Partisan - When something relates to all political parties or no particular political parties. A non-partisan election is one where candidates are not affiliated with particular parties and their party is not listed on the ballot. A non-partisan organization is one that associates with either no political parties or many different political parties, avoiding the association with one particular party.

Opinion Leaders - Opinion leaders are people in the community who can influence others. These people can be leaders of civic organizations, other political leaders, members of the media, or well-known and respected individuals. It is often important to win the endorsement of these individuals early in the campaign. See Endorsements.

Opponents - These are other candidates running for the same office and on the same ballot as your candidate.

Opposition Research - Opposition research is all the information, both good and bad, that your campaign can put together on all of the viable opponents. This is part of the overall research that should be done at the beginning of the campaign. See Research.

Paid Media - Any advertisements the campaign pays to have placed in the mass media, such as television, radio or newspapers.

Palm Card - A standard piece of campaign literature used to describe the candidate and provide a reason to vote for them. This should provide a clear summary of the campaign message. See Campaign Literature and Message.

Partisan - Anything relating to the political party. When an election is partisan, it means that party affiliation matters and may be listed on the ballot. See Non-Partisan.

Past Performance - This is the information for past elections on how many votes or what percentage of votes candidates from a particular party or similar ideology received. If there are similar candidates or multiple elections, the various percentages can be averaged together to find an overall performance.

People - One of the three resources every political campaign has, the other two being time and money. It is important to determine how many people will be needed to accomplish each activity and plan for it. See Campaign Resources.

Persuadable Voters - Voters who do not vote in a consistent way, voting for one candidate and not voting for a candidate with a similar ideology or from the same party in either the same election or in two consecutive elections. It is believed that these voters do not identify with a particular party or ideology and can be persuaded by a clear message.

Persuadability - This is the percentage of voters in a constituency, precinct or district that do not vote in a consistent way. In other words, voters in a district may vote for one candidate and not vote for a candidate with a similar ideology or from the same party in either the same election or in two consecutive elections. These non-consistent voters are considered to be persuadable and the percentage of persuadable voters in a district can influence the amount and type of voter contact the campaign plans in that district.

Phone Bank - A place where there are a number of phones and volunteers are able to come together as a group to phone voters.

Phoning - A method of voter contact in which volunteers call voters on the phone. This method can be used to persuade voters, identify supporters and turn out the vote near Election Day.

Platform - The program, often written, that the political party or candidate will address if and when they are elected. This is not a campaign message. See Program.

Plurality - The most votes cast in a given election. This differs from a majority of the votes cast or 50% plus one vote. See Majority.

Political Landscape - The environment in which the campaign will be waged, particularly in reference to the various people involved in politics in the area.

Political Players - Those people involved in politics in the area and who may influence the campaign one way or another.

Political Polling - Scientific, quantitative sociological research based on randomly selected voters used by the campaign to determine the opinions of the voters and used to provide strategic planning information.

Polling Place - The particular location where voters go to cast their ballots.

Posters - Large signs with the candidate's name on them and the office they are seeking which can be put in windows and on poles. Posters are good for increasing name recognition of the candidate and reminding people to vote. See Visibility.

Precinct - The smallest district or area in relation to elections. A precinct may be grouped into wards or polling units.

Precinct Captain - An individual responsible for organizing the party activity, voter contact program and Election Day operation in a particular precinct. Sometimes these people are volunteers and sometimes they are elected. Synonymous to Polling Booth Agent.

Precinct Information - Whatever information can be gathered about a particular precinct, such as voter list, turnout from the last election, and returns from the last election.

Preset Events - Any event or large grouping of voters organized outside the campaign, where the campaign can go and meet voters. These can be parades, conventions, rallies or debates. These are often outside the control of the campaign. See Created Events.

Press - Anyone working for a mass media organization and who is writing or otherwise commenting on the election campaign. This may also refer to what is written; example, "he received good press."

Press Conference - An event planned by the campaign to which the press is invited with the purpose to providing information about the campaign or on a particular issue.

Press Packet - A pack of information developed by the campaign and giving to the press to provide them with more information about the candidate and the campaign. A press packet often includes a candidate biography, a photo of the candidate, a copy of the press release announcing their candidacy or the speech, press releases outlining various position papers, copies of good press the campaign has received, and copies of campaign literature.

Press Q&A - An opportunity for the press to ask the candidate questions and receive answers.

Press Release - Information provided by the campaign to reporters and others in the mass media presenting the candidates position on a particular issue or event. Press releases are often written in the form of a news story.

Press Secretary - This is the individual in the campaign organization responsible for dealing with the mass media. See Mass Media and Press.

Print Media - Print media are independent newspapers and magazines or any other part of the mass media using the written word and/or still pictures, as opposed to the electronic media that use the spoken word and/or video. See Electronic Media and Mass Media.

Proactive Campaign - A campaign that has a strategy and a written plan to carry that strategy out. This campaign sets the agenda in the election and knows what to expect from their opponents. See Reactive Campaign.

Program - The candidate or party's program is "what they say they will do" concerning various issues important to the voters. A program is not a message. See Message and Platform.

Pull - Making sure that voters who support the candidate go to the polls and vote for the candidate on Election Day. The campaign should do everything short of "pulling" the voters to the polls. Generally only supporters who have been identified previously are encouraged to vote, except in areas of extreme support. See GOTV and Blind Pull.

Q&A - "Questions and Answers." See Press Q&A.

Race - An election campaign is often compared to a running race in which candidates "run for office." See Running for Office.

Reactive Campaign - A campaign that spends its resources responding to the political landscape and what happens during the campaign. This is a campaign that lacks a plan, is always behind and cannot set the agenda. See Proactive Campaign.

Research - All the information that will influence this election that your campaign can find. This may include information about the election rules, the constituency or the district, the voters, past elections, this election, your candidate and any viable opponents. Research is the first step in putting together a campaign strategy and plan.

Rule of Finite Resources - Every decision to do something is a decision not to do something else. Every campaign has a limited number of each of the resources, time, money and people, and must make decisions about how to use those resources. It is therefore important to have a written campaign plan which lays out the strategy.

Run Off - In certain systems, an election held to determine a winner with a majority of the votes when none of the candidates received a majority in the first round. The top two candidates who received the most votes in the first round will run in the run-off election.

Running for Office - An election campaign is often compared to a running race in which candidates "run for office." See Race.

Scheduler - The person in the campaign responsible for keeping the campaign calendar, the candidate's calendar and responding to invitations.

Single Mandate - An election constituency or district in which one candidate will win the position sought in this campaign.

Slogan - This is a short phrase that voters may remember to identify the candidate or campaign. A slogan is not a message.

Sound Trucks - Automobiles with loud speakers attached to them that go through areas of the constituency or district broadcasting a message. These are considered part of the visibility method of voter contact.

Special Election - An election not held at the usually scheduled time, often to fill a vacancy in the office. There is often a much lower voter turnout in a special or by-election. See By-Election.

Speech - Usually prepared remarks given orally to a group of people or a large audience.

Stay On Message - When a candidate or campaign continues to deliver the same message or theme at every opportunity. Often the opponent will try to pull the campaign off their message but it is critical not to let this happen.

Strategic Planning Session – A meeting, or short series of meetings, of the candidate and any key advisors that will gather the necessary information and determine the overall strategy of the campaign. This strategy must be written down in the form of a campaign plan. See Campaign Plan.

Strategy - The method, written into the campaign plan, of what the campaign will do from this point to Election Day to elect the candidate to the chosen office.

Stump Speech - A standard speech delivered by a candidate on many occasions. This speech should contain the campaign message as its core and be repeated at every opportunity.

Supporters - Voters and others who have been identified by the campaign as people who will vote for the candidate or party in this election.

Surrogate - Anyone speaking on behalf of the candidate or otherwise officially representing the candidate.

Swing District - An election district has a history of voting for different parties or different types of candidates in the same or consecutive elections. Because the district or constituency can "swing" back and forth between different parties or candidates, it is often important to spend campaign resources to persuade voters in these districts or constituencies to ensure that the campaign wins them. See Persuasiveness.

Swing Precincts - Precincts within a particular election constituency or district that have a history of voting for different parties or different ideologies in different elections. The campaign may want to put extra resources into these districts to ensure that the candidate wins them. See Precincts.

Swing Voter - Voters who are not tied to a particular political party or ideology, but have a history of voting for different parties or different ideologies in the same or different elections. These voters are considered persuadable and likely to be reached by a good campaign message or other information. See Persuadable Voter.

Target Voters - Voters whom the campaign believes are most likely to be persuaded by the campaign's message and thus provide the margin of victory. See Message and Margin of Victory.

Targeting - The process of dividing the voting population into smaller groups and determining which of the votes you want to concentrate your message on to provide the margin of victory. See demographic targeting and geographic targeting.

The Campaign - This refers to either the organization put together to elect a particular candidate or the period of time in which an election is waged.

Time - One of the three resources every political campaign has, the other two being people and money. It is important to determine how much time each campaign activity will take and plan for it. Unlike the other two resources, time is the same for each of the campaigns involved in an election, but not all campaigns use their time as effectively. See Campaign Resources.

Tracking Poll - A political poll taken later in the campaign to determine how the campaign's message and the various methods of voter contact is affecting undecided and persuadable voters. See Baseline Poll and Political Poll.

Turnout - This is the portion of the electorate that actually goes to the polls and votes. This can be referred to as a percentage or as a real number.

Values - The principles considered desirable by the voters.

Visibility - The voter contact method in which the candidate's name is advertised on signs, tee shirts and cups, and just about anything else. If seen enough this can often raise the candidates name recognition but it does little to persuade voters with a campaign message.

Volunteer - A supporter of the candidate who generally spends some of their time helping the campaign without being paid a salary.

Volunteer Coordinator - A person on the campaign staff responsible for recruiting and scheduling volunteers.

Vote Shifting - When voters vote for one candidate in one election and vote for a candidate from a different party or with a different ideology in the next election. Voters who shift their votes are considered to be persuadable with a campaign message. See Persuadability.

Vote Splitting - When voters vote for one candidate and vote for a candidate from a different party or with a different ideology on the same ballot in the same election. Voters who split their votes are considered to be persuadable with a campaign message. See Persuadability.

Voter Drop Off - Less important or lower profile races often receive less votes than higher profile races because often voters do not know about the race, do not know the candidates and do not feel comfortable voting for candidates they do not know.

Voter Fatigue - The tendency of voters not to vote for candidates they do not know or in races they do not care about. Voter fatigue is greatest in low profile or down ballot races. See Voter Drop Off, Low Profile and Down Ballot.

Voter File - A database that contains at least the name and address of all the voters in a constituency or district. An enhanced voter file may have other information about the voters such as their phone numbers, their ages, and whether or not they have a history of voting in the past. Political parties and candidates may further enhance the voter file by finding out who supports the candidate or what issues are important to voters. The only way to do this is to ask voters directly.

Voter Priorities - Voters often care about things that affect them directly, such as their job or the education of their children. They often care less about policy issues that they have little control over. Candidates need to speak to the voters about things they care about.

Voter - This is any person who is able to vote in this election for this particular office. See Electorate.

APPENDIX B

POLITICAL CAMPAIGN
RESEARCH QUESTIONS

These are a series of questions designed to assist the campaign in understanding the particular situation of the campaign and develop a realistic strategy. Not every question may apply to every type of campaign but by working through the entire series you may begin to think about things you may have overlooked.

Some questions you will know the answer immediately and others will require some research. In some cases, you may have to take an educated guess about the answer to a particular question. You should do this only as a last resort. It is important that you set and stick to a time limit for completing this research and answering these questions.

1. Election Rules

A. The Type of Election

> ➤ What type of election is this (for example, party list or candidate, single mandate or multi mandate)?
> ➤ What is required to win the election (for example, a simple plurality or a majority of the votes cast)?
> ➤ How many seats are open in this election race (for example, is this a single mandate or multi-mandate seat)?
> ➤ Will you be running alone or as part of a team?

➢ What are the roles and responsibilities of the office you are running for?

B. Election Law

Filing Candidacy
❖ What are the filing deadlines?
❖ What is needed to file as a candidate?

Campaign Finance
❖ Are there contribution limits?
❖ What requirements are there for reporting contributions?
❖ What are the campaign finance filing deadlines?

Campaigning
❖ What is the law regarding access to the media and time to go to media?
❖ What is the law regarding sound trucks, posters, billboards, lawn signs or other methods of visibility?

Election Day
❖ Is there a turnout requirement for the election to be valid?
❖ When do the polls open and close?
❖ What are the rules about campaigning on Election Day?
❖ What are the rules about campaigning near a polling place?
❖ Who is responsible for running the elections and validating the results?
❖ Is there a history of voter fraud in the area?

2. The Constituency or District

A. What is the constituency or district like?

➢ What are the physical boundaries of the constituency or district (in other words, how large is the district)?
➢ What are the physical characteristics of the constituency or district (for example, is the district rural or urban, flat or mountainous, etc.)?
➢ Are there any important environmental factors affecting the constituency or district?
➢ What is the economic situation in the constituency or district?

➤ Have the economic circumstances recently changed for the better or worse?

➤ How has the overall population of the constituency or district changed recently?

➤ What is the transportation system like?

➤ What other data is available on the constituency or district?

B. What is the political landscape of the constituency or district?

➤ Who are the political players in the constituency or district?

➤ What is the situation with the local, regional or national political parties?

➤ Who are the civic leaders?

➤ Who are the business leaders?

➤ Who else could be considered an opinion leader?

C. Where do voters get their information?

➤ Who, what and where are all the local media outlets?

➤ Who controls the local media outlets?

➤ Who are the reporters covering this election for the local media outlets?

➤ When are the news programs?

➤ What are the deadlines for the reporters?

➤ How do the media view the campaign?

➤ How will the media cover the campaign?

➤ Which press will be favorable to the candidate and which will be favorable to the opposition?

➤ Where can the campaign buy advertisements?

3. The Voters

❖ Is there a voter file or accurate list of all possible voters in the constituency or district and who has it?

❖ What is the party breakdown of the voters or level of support for various political parties?

- ❖ What are the demographic make-up of the voters (for example, income levels, education levels, professions, race or ethnic backgrounds, religious background, age, gender, etc.)?
- ❖ What is the geographic break down of the voting population (who lives where)?
- ❖ Which groups of voters are more likely to vote than other groups of voters?
- ❖ What are your supporters like?
- ❖ What are the target voters like and how many meet this profile?
- ❖ What are the important organizations in the constituency or district?
- ❖ What are the major forms of recreation?
- ❖ Where do people work?
- ❖ Where do people shop?
- ❖ Do certain demographic groups, such as seniors, students or apartment dwellers tend to live in a particular part of the constituency or district?
- ❖ Have there been any substantial changes in the overall make-up of the population recently?

4. Past Elections

- ❖ Who ran for this position in past elections?
- ❖ What where the results for this position in past elections?
- ❖ What percentage of the population voted in past elections?
- ❖ How many votes were cast in past elections?
- ❖ How many votes were needed to win this position in past elections?
- ❖ What are the results for elections for other positions in this constituency or district?
- ❖ What is the difference in level of support similar candidates received in past elections?

5. This Election

A. The Issues

- ➢ What local issues are important to voters?
- ➢ What regional or national issues are important to voters?
- ➢ What is the main motivating factor for voters?

➢ What is the voter mood?

➢ How do the voters feel about the Party leaders?

➢ How do the voters feel about the national leaders?

B. Other Races

➢ What other races will be on the ballot in this election and how does their presence impact this race?

➢ Who else will have campaign organizations operating in the constituency or district?

➢ What opportunities are there for coordinating with other campaigns?

6. Our Candidate

A. What is your candidate's background?

❖ Describe the candidate's childhood.

❖ Describe the candidate's education.

❖ Describe the candidate's work history.

❖ Describe the candidate's immediate family.

❖ What role will the family play in the campaign?

❖ Has the candidate previously held elected or appointed public office?

❖ What public statements or important votes has the candidate made?

❖ What have others said about the candidate (both good and bad)?

❖ Does the candidate have a record of keeping past promises?

❖ Is there a particular voting group that is either happy or unhappy with the candidate?

❖ Is there any court or other public records of the candidate?

❖ What is the candidate's voting record and can this be made public?

❖ What is the candidate best known for and how well known is the candidate?

❖ What are the most important accomplishments of the candidate?

❖ Is the candidate charismatic when meeting people? Is the candidate a good public speaker?

❖ Are there any negative things in the candidate's past which the campaign should deal with or which an opponent might take advantage of?

B. What resources does the candidate or the campaign have?

> What financial resources will the candidate use?
> How much time will the candidate realistically spend fundraising?
> To what organizations does the candidate belong?
> What assistance can these organizations provide?
> What organizations or political action committees are likely to donate to the campaign?
> What is the cheapest way to raise the most money from proven and potential contributors?
> Is there early money?
> When will the money come in?
> What is the cash flow for the campaign?
> When will the contributions be collected and how will this affect cash flow?

C. What does the candidate like and dislike?

7. Viable Opponents

A. Who are the viable opponents?

B. What are the viable opponents' backgrounds?

❖ Describe the opponents' education.
❖ Describe the opponents' previous jobs.
❖ Describe the opponents' previous elected or appointed positions.
❖ What is the opponents' voting record?
❖ What previous public statements or important votes have the opponents' made?
❖ Are there courts or other public records on the opponents?
❖ What negative thing in the opponents' background could be exploited?

C. What resources do the opponents bring to the campaign?

❖ How will the opponents fund their campaign?
❖ What other resources are available to the opponents?

APPENDIX C

+———————————————————+

GEOGRAPHIC TARGETING METHODOLOGY

This appendix lays out the methodology for measuring the three characteristics important in geographic targeting as explained in Step Three: Targeting the Voters.

Turnout is, quite simply, the percent of eligible voters who actually vote. Because, your only clue to a precinct's or ward's behavior in the upcoming election, is its behavior in past elections. You generally predict turnout with the following formula:

(Votes Cast 1 plus Votes Cast 2) divided by (Eligible Voters times 2 elections)

Votes Cast 1 = Number of votes cast in first past election

Votes Cast 2 = Number of votes cast in second past election

Eligible Voters = Total number of eligible voters in the precinct or polling unit

Thus, this formula is simply the average turnout over two past elections. People doing very careful targeting will give more weight in their formulas to more recent elections.

In measuring expected turnout, it is important that you choose elections of a similar character to the upcoming election.

Performance is the percent of voters in a precinct who consistently vote for candidates or parties of the same orientation as your candidate. In places with strong party affiliation, this may mean looking at the average of all the votes received by all of the candidates of the same party over the course of two or more elections. The following formula would be used to define a precinct's "performance:"

(DemLeg95 plus DemPres96 plus DemGov97 plus DemChair97) divided by 4 Elections

DemLeg95 = percentage of votes received by "Democratic Party" legislative candidate in the precinct in 1995

DemPres96 = percentage of votes received by "Democratic Party" presidential candidate in the precinct in 1996

DemGov97 = percentage of votes received by "Democratic Party" governor candidate in the precinct in 1997

DemChair97 = percentage of votes received by "Democratic Party" Council Chairman candidate in the precinct in 1997

This formula is a simple average of the performance in the precinct of four "Democratic Party" candidates in four elections. Performance formulas are usually more complex, and, again, people doing more careful targeting will give more weight to more recent elections.

Obviously, defining "performance" in areas where party affiliations are less strong will be a little trickier. One possible formula might be:

(demLeg95 plus demPres96 plus demGov97 plus demChair97) divided by 4 Elections

demLeg95 = percentage of votes received by a similar "democratic" oriented legislative candidate in the precinct in 1995

demPres96 = percentage of votes received by a similar "democratic" oriented presidential candidate in the precinct in 1996

demGov97 = percentage of votes received by a similar "democratic" oriented governor candidate in the precinct in 1997

demChair97 = percentage of votes received by a similar "democratic" oriented Council Chairman candidate in the precinct in 1997

This formula is the average of the votes for "democratic orientation" in four elections. Obviously, choosing which parties and which candidates represent "democratic orientation" will be a little tricky.

Persuadability is the percentage of voters in a precinct that do not vote in a consistent way. Either they "split" their vote (vote for candidates of different orientations in the same election) or "shift" their vote (vote for candidates of different orientations over the course of two or more elections). It is generally considered that "vote splitters" and "vote shifters" are the voters most likely to be persuaded by a campaign's efforts.

A campaign might use the following formula to measure Persuadability. This formula averages the precinct's "vote shifters" (between the legislative races in 1995 and the presidential races in 1996) with the "vote splitters" (between the gubernatorial race and Council Chair race in 1997).

[(DemLeg95 minus DemPres96) plus (DemGov97 minus Dem Chair 97)] divided by 2 Elections

DemLeg95 = number of votes received by "Democratic Party" legislative candidate in the precinct in 1995

DemPres96 = number of votes received by "Democratic Party" presidential candidate in the precinct in 1996

DemGov97 = number of votes received by "Democratic Party" governor candidate in the precinct in 1997

DemChair97 = number of votes received by "Democratic Party" council Chair candidate in the precinct in 1997

Use absolute values for the subtraction results.

Again, where party affiliations are less strong; defining "Persuadability" will be a little trickier. One possible formula might be:

[(demLeg95 minus demPres96) plus (demGov97 minus dem Chair 97)] divided by 2 Elections

demLeg95 = number of votes received by a similar "democratic" oriented legislative candidate in the precinct in 1995

demPres96 = number of votes received by a similar "democratic" oriented presidential candidate in the precinct in 1996

demGov97 = number of votes received by a similar "democratic" oriented governor candidate in the precinct in 1997

demChair97 = number of votes received by a similar "democratic" oriented council Chair candidate in the precinct in 1997

This formula averages the precinct's "vote shifters" (between the legislative races in 1995 and the presidential races in 1996) with the "vote splitters" (between the gubernatorial race and council Chair race in 1997) for "democratic orientation" in four elections. Obviously, choosing which parties and which candidates represent "democratic orientation" will be a little tricky.

APPENDIX D

ISSUES RELATED TO POLITICAL POLLING

Goals of Polling

Strategic information for political campaign

The chief goal of polling is to provide you with strategic planning information that is useful for conducting its political campaign. Specifically, you must use your polls to find out which demographic groups are most likely to be your supporters and will be persuaded by your message. Polling simply to find out the current standing of the candidate is useless and a waste of valuable resources. The campaign should conduct each poll with a specific purpose, and should have a specific reason for asking each question on the poll.

Discover the attitudes and concerns of voters

A political campaign is about voters. To be successful, you must talk about the things in which voters are interested in a way that voters can relate to. Polling is an excellent way to measure the attitudes and concerns of voters.

Discover the issues that move voters

Every political activist knows the major issues of the current political campaign. However, given limited resources with which to meet voters, the campaign must know the priorities of the voters among these issues, especially how those priorities differ among sub-sets of the voting population. Polling can help the campaign focus its message and make the best use of its resources.

Discover the candidate's position

Voters perceive each candidate to have its own strengths and weaknesses; a candidate that is perceived to be strongly against corruption, for example, may simultaneously be perceived as weak in dealing with economic or foreign policy. The campaign can use polling to discover exactly where it stands in the minds of the voters and to determine on what issues to focus its campaign.

Test messages

The campaign can use polling to determine the effectiveness of various messages before committing resources toward communicating those messages to voters. Additionally, you can use polling to determine the effectiveness of the messages that opponents are likely to use against them, as well as the best defenses against those messages.

Track trends

As the campaign progresses, you need to know what is happening in the minds of the voters: are they listening to the candidate's messages or to messages of the opponents? Small-scale "tracking polls" can determine this information during the election campaign.

Types of Questions:

Screening questions

Since the purpose of the poll is to formulate election strategy, you should be interested in talking only to those who will actually vote. Political polls typically begin with a set of screening questions to determine who is most likely to vote.

Favorability questions

The campaign needs to determine which parties, leaders, and institutions are viewed favorably or unfavorably by voters. The voter must be encouraged to be honest, to admit that he does not know a name nor has opinion; often, a fake "control" name is used for this purpose.

Questions about the general political environment

These questions might include: "Is the country on the right track or the wrong track?" or "Are you better off or worse off now than you were several years ago?" The purpose of such questions is to estimate the overall mood and attitudes of the voters.

Issue importance and positioning questions

These questions ask voters to prioritize the political issues to be discussed in the campaign and to evaluate the parties' performance on these issues. In one variant, voters are asked to rate each issue (crime, inflation, unemployment, etc.) as "extremely important", "very important", "somewhat important", or "not very important"; in another variant, voters are actually asked to prioritize short lists of issues.

Leadership qualities and positioning questions

These questions ask voters to prioritize the characteristics that they wish to see in their political leaders. The wording of these questions is similar to that of the issue importance questions, substituting phrases like "strong", "well-educated", or "understands people like me" for the issue terms.

Horse race questions

Horse-race questions are quite familiar: "If the election were held today, would you vote for Lucky or Success?" While important for tracking progress, these questions are in some sense the least important questions on the poll. Because a small percentage of voters may identify with parties or candidates, more useful to candidates are questions about whether voters would consider voting for Y candidate or party; this way potential supporters can be identified by demographic groups.

Message testing questions

Message testing questions might include: "Would you be more likely or less likely to vote for a candidate/party with Y characteristics?" The purpose, of course, is to test both the party's and the party's opponents' messages to determine their likely effect.

These questions are often worded neutrally to mask the name of the party or candidate being discussed.

Two-sided issue questions

The purpose of these questions is to find out what voters might think about a particular issue after hearing arguments from both sides. A typical question might be: "Proponents of a certain proposal say X, while opponents of the proposal say Y. Do you strongly agree with the proposal, mildly agree with the proposal, mildly disagree, or strongly disagree?"

Demographic questions

At the end of a poll, voters are usually asked a series of demographic questions (age, income level, education level, occupation etc.) to determine what differences exist among sub-sets of the population. This is important for defining the demographic groups who are supporting your party, undecided, or supporting your opponents. This is also the key to defining issues and messages that work for demographic groups.

Common Mistakes in Design and Use of Polls

Bad sampling

The sample of the poll must be completely random and must reflect the population that will ultimately vote. Too many or not enough respondents from one sex, age, income, or geographic group, etc. will give inaccurate information about the population as a whole. Screening is critical to ensure that only likely voters respond.

Biased questions

The purpose of the poll is to give the party accurate information. Thus, all questions must be worded in a neutral, non-biased manner in order to get the most honest response.

Asking two questions at once

Asking two questions at once will give you confusing answers. A single point and direct question is considered suitable.

Insider questions

Faulty polls often include questions that are well understood by politicians but not by average people. If the respondent does not understand a question, he cannot give an honest response.

Questions too general

Everyone knows that the economy is an important issue in any political campaign. But what exactly about the economy is important? The questions in a poll must be specific to the issues that will be important.

Over-reliance on horse race questions

The answer to a horse-race question is ultimately important only on Election Day. A party should never become over-confident from strong poll results or despondent from weak poll results. Rather, the party should use the poll to determine its strategy for the future.

Failure to use cross-tab information to target messages to voter segments

Voters are not uniform and will not respond in the same way to the same messages. The party should use the poll to find out the differences among sub-sets of voters and to design messages for each target sub-set.

APPENDIX E

DRAWING CONTRAST WITH YOUR OPPONENTS

One of the most difficult problems facing candidates and political activists is the problem of creating a contrast with your opponents in the minds of the voters. Party programs and messages tend to be bland and generic, and the voters never understand why one candidate or party is better than another. As a result, voters grow cynical and begin to view democratic elections as meaningless.

In designing your campaign message, you must give your target audience the sharpest possible contrast with your opponents. If you do not, then your target audience has no reason to vote for you instead of your opponent. In order to ensure that your message has this contrast, you should be able to word it in the following way:

"When you go to the polls on Election Day, I want you to keep one thing in mind. The differences between my opponent and me could not be clearer. You can vote for me, who stands for AX, or you can vote for my opponents, who stand for BY. What our country and our region/zone need are a lot more AX and a lot less BY. That is what this election is about, and that is what you are going to decide."

When searching for the "AX" and "BY", you may look at the following areas:

- ❖ Values: How is what you stand for significantly different than what your opponents stand for?
- ❖ Policies: What would you do as an elected leader that is significantly different from what your opponents would do?
- ❖ Experience: How will the differences between your work and educational experience and your opponents' experience influence the way you would behave in office? Often, when values and policies are very similar, experience is the best way to draw contrast - Which candidate is best able to deliver the promised policies or values?

For any particular trait under the above headings, you must craft your message in order to draw the most favorable contrast with your opponents. Examples of how to do this include:

AX	Vs.	BY
Values		**Values**
Positive change **Or** **Stability, certainty**	Vs.	Stagnancy, status quo, Or Instability, uncertainty
Mainstream **Or** **Bold, dynamic**	Vs.	Fringe, radical, extreme, Or Staid, unwilling to risk
Patriotic **Or** **Common sense**	Vs.	Unpatriotic, Or Nationalist extremism
Pragmatic, compromising **Or** **Idealistic**	Vs.	Partisan, uncompromising, Or "Sell-out"
For the common people **Or** **Based on intelligence**	Vs.	For the elite Or Anti-intellectual
Optimistic **Or** **Realist**	Vs.	Pessimistic, Or Dreamer
Honest, trustworthy **Or** **Realistic, world-wise**	Vs.	Corrupt, untrustworthy, Or Naive, "babe-in-the-woods"

Policies		
Protects your region first **Or** **Statesman looking out for the** **Nation**	Vs.	Sell-out to Nation, Or Provincial, small-minded
Against greedy businessmen **Or** **Pro-business, pro-growth**	Vs.	In the pocket of the rich, Or Over-regulation, Anti-growth
Social protection **Or** **For individual responsibility**	Vs.	Uncaring, heartless, Or For the narcotic of government support
Individual thinker **Or** **Trusted "team player"**	Vs.	Puppet of party leader, Or Maverick, "loose cannon"
For responsible public **investment** **Or** **For private initiative**	Vs.	Allowing factories to deteriorate, Or For support of inefficient wasteful state enterprises
For quick and efficient **privatization** **Or** **For fairness in distributing** **assets**	Vs.	For continued inefficient management Or For giving national resources to the rich and corrupt

Experience		
Young, dynamic **Or** **Wisdom, experienced**	Vs.	Old, stuck in the past Or Foolish, inexperienced
Has the clout to get things **done** **Or** **Independent, integrity**	Vs.	Weak, not serious Or Has ties to corrupt nomenclature
Highly educated and **intelligent** **Or** **Understands common people**	Vs.	Unimpressive background Or Egg headed, out of touch

Extensive government experience Or Real-world experience	Vs.	Untried, untested Or Part of the problem in the Country
Understands business Or Not corrupted by money	Vs.	Locked in the past system Or Tainted by money

Source: National Democratic Institute for International Affairs (2009).

APPENDIX F

SAMPLE CAMPAIGN FORMS

As the campaign becomes more intense, it is important that you have established procedures for keeping accurate records, delivering clear instructions and dealing with various things such as invitations and contributions to your campaign. You should review the following forms and consider adapting them for use in your campaign.

Sample Volunteer Card or Database Form

Voter's Name: _____

Address: _____

Precinct/Ward/Polling Unit: _____

Phone: _____

Party Affiliation: _____

Needs:

More Information

Absentee Ballot

Ride to the Polls

Election Day Child Care

Will support the campaign by:

Volunteering

Canvassing

Working to Get Out The Vote

Making a Donation

Phoning

Additional Information: _____

_____

Supervisor's Instructions for Phone Bank

- ❖ As supervisor of the phone bank, you will be responsible for all the phoning activity, and the general productivity of the bank.
- ❖ You will be calling from lists of voters in the targeted precincts/ward/polling unit. The phone bank coordinator will present phoning lists to you.
- ❖ You will be responsible for keeping your phones filled during all phoning hours.
- ❖ You will need to hold a training session for your volunteers the first time. This need only last about one half-hour. Rehearse the phone message with them, instruct them in making the tally sheets, etc.
- ❖ Be pleasant and courteous. Encourage your volunteers constantly. Reward good performance and be watchful for trouble areas for those making the calls.
- ❖ It is your responsibility to total all tally sheets and compute the statistical evaluation sheets. Do this at the end of the shift.
- ❖ Run shifts. Assign phone volunteers on a shift basis each day.
- ❖ Collect special request forms periodically. Do not let them pile up. Refer them to whoever will do the follow-up with more information about the candidate.
- ❖ Most phoning should take place during the evening hours (5:30 PM to 9:30 PM) and all day Saturday (10:00 AM to 9:00 PM). Daytime phoning during the week is an option, particularly if you are falling behind schedule.

Sample ID Telephone Script

"Good evening (morning or afternoon). May I speak with Mr./Ms. _____, please?

Mr. /Ms. _____, my name is _____ and calling from Change Consulting. We're conducting a survey to determine the choice of voters in this area. If the election for legislature were held today, would you vote for _____ or _____? Thank you for your time."

Rate the voters on the phone sheets according to the following scale:

"1" Supports your candidate

"2" Undecided

"3" Supports an opponent

Do not get into discussions with the voters. This will only take time away from making more calls. Only answer the most basic questions and do not discuss issues.

Remember to thank each individual spoken to when concluding the call.

Turn in your completed call sheets when finished. If you do not complete a call sheet, make sure it is clearly marked at the point you stopped. Keep any call sheets you did not complete separate.

Thank you for your effort in making your phone bank a success.

Sample Canvass Instruction Sheet

What you are doing

We are canvassing homes in swing ward to tell voters about our candidate and give them a piece of campaign literature and answer their questions.

We also want to register their preferences in this very important race. When the canvass is finished, the campaign will be delivering more literature to undecided voters.

How to do it

This kit contains everything you will need:

The survey sheets - make sure you record the name, address/phone line and preference of the voters. A"1" supports your candidate, A"2" is undecided and A"3" supports the opponent.

The volunteer/canvasser badge - wearing this badge will identify you as a campaign volunteer/ canvasser.

The candidate-briefing sheet - this will tell you about the candidate and what they stand for.

Campaign Brochures - give one of these to each voter.

The Q Slip - When you get a question you cannot answer, do not fake it. Just tell the voter that you are a volunteer/ canvasser, that you do not know the answer but that you will find out and get them the answer. Then fill out a "Q Slip" which will be processed at the campaign headquarters.

The Report - When you have finished, please fill out the Canvass Report so that you are able to quickly tally the results of the canvass and gage your progress.

What to say

Remember that you are a personal Representative of the candidate. The words you say and the impression you make will have a big effect on the voter's decision.

Here is an outline of the canvassing message. You will need to go over it a few times to get it down in your own words.

Identify yourself

"Good afternoon, my name is (your name), and I'm a volunteer/ canvasser for (candidate), who is running for Legislative or Gubernatorial position. May I speak with you for just a moment?"

Talk about the candidate

"I'm working for (candidate) because (candidate) is an honest candidate with a good record of helping people in your community. I think that (candidate) is one of the few candidates you can trust these days."

Ask for question

"We are conducting a people to people campaign because (candidate) wants to make sure the people know where (candidate) stands on the issues. Is there a particular issue you are concerned about?

Offer brochure

"Have you made up your mind about the election, (Mr. /Ms. Voter)?" (If yes, determine their preference and conclude the conversation appropriately. In no, continue.)

"I would like to leave this brochure with you to tell you more about (candidate). Please consider voting for (candidate) on Election Day - (candidate) will be a great member of Legislature. Thank you for your time."

Special guidelines

You will find that almost everyone will be polite and willing to listen. If you contact an unfriendly person, do not argue - just terminate the conversation quickly.

If you have questions or problems; call (coordinator) at (phone number).

Sample Canvass Report

Rating System: "1" - Supporter, "2" - Leaning toward Candidate, "3" - Undecided, "4" - Unfavorable, "5" - Supporting Opponent, "R" - Refused to Answer, "X" - Not at Home. Street Name: _____ Community: _____ Precinct/Ward: _____ Polling Place: _____					
House #	Voter's Name	Phone #	Rating	Comments	Follow Up

Source: National Democratic Institute for International Affairs (2009).

Sample "Dear Friend" Card

> Dear Friend,
>
> Next Tuesday you have the opportunity to elect a new member of Legislature who will be more effective at representing us in the Assembly.
>
> I'm voting for (candidate) because he will work for better schools for all of your children. Please join me and vote for (candidate).
>
> Sincerely,
>
> (Volunteer's signature)

Sample Scheduling Form

Date of Request:	Accept:
Decision Made:	Reject:
Date of Response:	Hold:
Event:	
Date:	
Time:	
Location:	
Sponsoring Organization:	
Address:	
Phone:	
Contact Person:	
Address:	
Phone:	
Description of Program:	
Number Expected to Attend:	
Will Media Be Present?	
Nature of Candidate's Participation:	
Other Information:	

Sample Fundraising Form

Potential Donor Sheet

Name: _____

Business: _____

Address: _____

Work phone: _____ Home phone: _____ Email: _____

Interest in giving: _____

Contact to ask: _____

Ask for how much: _____

Notes of contact/calls/responses: _____

Follow-up: _____

APPENDIX G

STRATEGIC CAMPAIGN PLAN TEMPLATE

The following template is designed to help you pull all the information you have gathered together in one place and develop a comprehensive campaign plan. Much of the information should be compiled in the answers to the worksheets found within this manual.

Step One: Data Collection and Research

Briefly describe the Election Laws that will affect this election.

_____

_____

_____

Briefly describe the Constituency/District in which you will be running.

_____

_____

_____

Briefly describe the Voters in the constituency/district.

_____

_____

_____

Briefly describe what has happened in past elections in this constituency/ district.

_____

_____

_____

Briefly describe the factors that will influence this election.

_____

_____

_____

Briefly describe your Candidate.

_____

_____

_____

Briefly describe all the Viable Opponents.

_____

_____

_____

Step Two: Set a Goal

The total population of the constituency/district is:

_____

The total number of voters is:

_____

Expected turnout in this election is:

_____

We will be guaranteed victory if you receive this many votes:

_____

We will have to communicate your message to this many homes in order to achieve this number of votes:

_____

Step Three: Targeting the Voters

Geographic Targeting
Based on past elections, your candidate can expect to do well in these parts of the constituency/district (our base area):

_____

Based in past elections, the opposition can expect to do well in these parts of the constituency/district (their base area):

_____

Based on past elections, the following areas of the constituency/district will be the swing areas where you will have to persuade the balance of the voters you need to win:

_____

Demographic Targeting
Our candidate can be considered to belong to the following demographic groups, which will be our base of support:

_____
_____
_____

These other demographic groups can be expected to support our candidate for the following reasons:

_____
_____
_____

All of these demographic groups make up the following percentage of the population:

_____

In real numbers, this is the following number of votes:

_____

We can expect to receive the following percentage of these votes:

_____

In real numbers, this is the following number of votes:

_____

If need be, you can also attract votes from the following collateral groups:

_____

Our opponents can expect to attract their votes primarily from the following demographic groups:

_____

_____

_____

Voter Analysis
Members of your target audience share the following Values:

_____

_____

_____

Members of your target audience share the following Attitudes:

_____

_____

_____

Members of your target audience share concerns about the following Issues:

_____

_____

_____

Members of your target audience share the same desire for the following Leadership Qualities:

_____

Step Four: Determining and Developing the Campaign Message

The Message Box

What We Say About Us	What We Say About Them
What They Say About Us	What They Say About Them

The Campaign Message
The following is a one-minute statement that answers the question "why are you running for this office?"

_____

_____

_____

_____

_____

_____

_____

_____

_____

_____

The Message Check
This message meets all of the criteria:
- ❖ Is it short?
- ❖ Is it truthful and credible?
- ❖ Is it persuasive and important to voters?
- ❖ Does it show contrast with your opponents?
- ❖ Is it clear and does it speak to the heart?
- ❖ Is it directed at your target audience?

Does the following support your message?
- ❖ The candidates biography
- ❖ Stories about the candidate
- ❖ The campaign slogan
- ❖ The campaign logo
- ❖ Endorsements
- ❖ The party message

Key Issues of the Electorate

The following are the most important issues to your target audience:

_____

_____

_____

_____

_____

_____

_____

_____

Our campaign is best positioned to focus on the following issues and will relate them to the campaign message in the following way:

_____

_____

_____

_____

_____

_____

_____

_____

_____

_____

Step Five: Developing a Voter Contact Plan

In general, we intend to communicate our message to the voters using the following methods:

Demographic Group	Method to Reach Them

Source: National Democratic Institute for International Affairs (2009).

The following are your specific voter contact goals which, when achieved, will guarantee victory.

Description of Activity 1 with a Quantifiable Goal:

_____

_____

_____

_____

_____

Description of Activity 2 with a Quantifiable Goal:

_____

_____

_____

_____

_____

Description of Activity 3 with a Quantifiable Goal:

_____
_____
_____
_____
_____

Description of Activity 4 with a Quantifiable Goal:

_____
_____
_____
_____
_____

Description of Activity 5 with a Quantifiable Goal:

_____
_____
_____
_____
_____

Campaign Timeline

The following is your campaign timeline, which outlines all of the activities the campaign intends to complete. Each activity is assigned a coordinator, the number of people needed to complete the task, and a cost.

Date	Activity	Coordinator and Volunteers	Expenses
Election Day			
One Week Before Election Day			
Two Weeks Before Election Day			

Three Weeks Before Election Day		
Four Weeks Before Election Day		
Five Weeks Before Election Day		
Six Weeks Before		
Seven Weeks Before Election Day		
Eight Weeks Before Election Day		
Three Months Before Election Day		
Four Months Before Election Day		
Five Months Before Election Day		
Six Months Before Election Day		

Source: National Democratic Institute for International Affairs (2009).

Campaign Structure

These people will have the following roles in the campaign:

Name	Role	Phone Number

Campaign Budget

The total cost of the candidate's registration activities is:

_____

The total cost of all the voter contact activities is:

_____

The total administrative cost (headquarters, staff, office machines, etc.) is:

_____

The total research cost is:

_____

Adding all of these costs together, you will spend the following amount on this campaign:

_____

BIBLIOGRAPHY

National Democratic Institute for International Affairs (2009). Political Campaign Planning Manual, A step by step guide to winning elections, Washington, DC: NDI.

www.ingramcontent.com/pod-product-compliance
Lightning Source LLC
Chambersburg PA
CBHW020512290526
45786CB00002B/568